Walk routes researched and written by John Gillham, John Morrison and David Winpenny
Cycle routes researched and written by John Gillham and Jon Sparks
Series managing editor: David Hancock

Produced by AA Publishing
© Automobile Association Developments Limited 2005
First published 2005

Published by AA Publishing (a trading name of Automobile Association Developments Limited, whose registered office is Southwood East, Apollo Rise, Farnborough, Hampshire, GU14 0JW; registered number 1878835).

A02013

Ordnance Survey®   This product includes mapping data licensed from Ordnance Survey®
with the permission of the Controller of Her Majesty's Stationery Office.
© Crown copyright 2005. All rights reserved. Licence number 399221.

ISBN-10: 0-7495-4456-2
ISBN-13: 978-0-7495-4456-0

A CIP catalogue record for this book is available from the British Library.

The contents of this book are believed correct at the time of printing. Nevertheless, the publishers cannot be held responsible for any errors or omissions or for changes in the details given in this book or for the consequences of any reliance on the information it provides. We have tried to ensure accuracy in this book, but things do change and we would be grateful if readers would advise us of any inaccuracies they may encounter. This does not affect your statutory rights.

We have taken all reasonable steps to ensure that these walks and cycle rides are safe and achievable by people with a realistic level of fitness. However, all outdoor activities involve a degree of risk and the publishers accept no responsibility for any injuries caused to readers whilst following these walks and cycle rides. For advice on walking and cycling in safety, see pages 12 to 15.

Visit AA Publishing's website www.theAA.com/bookshop

Page layouts by pentacorbig, High Wycombe
Colour reproduction by Keene Group, Andover
Printed in Spain by Graficas Estella

AA

Pub Walks & Cycle Rides

Yorkshire and the Yorkshire Dales

Locator map

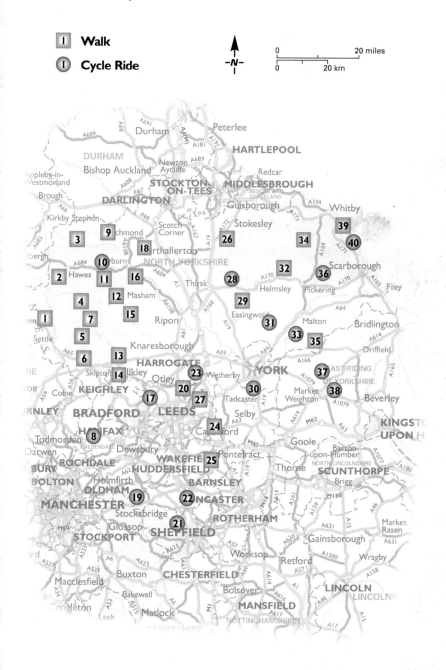

Walk

Cycle Ride

-N-

0   20 miles

0   20 km

Contents

Picture on page 4: The North York Moors National Park

Contents

Yorkshire and the Yorkshire Dales

The Yorkshire Dales receive thousands of visitors each year, most of whom are seeking peace and quiet on the moors and in the Dales. There's plenty of space for everyone, as Yorkshire and the Dales cover a large geographical area, with North Yorkshire alone, claiming the title of England's largest county.

The area has plenty to offer visitors, not least many naturally occuring phenomena such as the odd geological formation near Austwick known as the erratics, and the Wensleydale waterfalls Hardraw Force (England's highest unbroken waterfall) and Aysgarth Falls. You'll find Mallyan Spout waterfall at the beginning of the walk route which begins in Goathland.

In terms of the type of route you wish to follow, there are several 'official' trails which go through Yorkshire. Choose from the Pennine Way, the Coast-to-Coast route, the Trans-Pennine Trail, which is the country's first multi-user long-distance trail and is open to walkers and cyclists, or the

Many routes take in towns or villages. Hawes is known for producing crumbly Wensleydale cheese, Malham is one of the most well-visited villages in the Dales and West Burton is one of the region's prettiest villages. If you are looking to visit somewhere more out-of-the-way, Keld is one of the remoter villages. One cycle route goes to the regenerated village of Saltaire, which has stylish Salts Mill containing a gallery with works by Bradford-born artist David Hockney, cafés and opportunities for shopping.

There are plenty of other places to visit on route or after you've finished your walk or cycle. You can take in the impressive ruins of the priory at Bolton Abbey which are a mix of Norman and later styles, or the romantic ruins of Byland Abbey. Castles and magnificent estates abound in Yorkshire – choose from Middleham Castle, Richmond Castle, grand Harewood House on the edge of Leeds or, the pièce de résistance, Castle Howard, which could provide an entire day's worth of entertainment including grounds, shops, a plant centre and various places to eat. Other grand buildings with beautiful gardens include Wentworth Castle and Bramham Park. Alternatively, take a trip on the North Yorkshire Moors Railway or see extreme mountain bikers plunging down some very steep slopes in Wharncliffe Woods (joining in is optional).

And last but not least, the pubs. As this region is extremely popular with walkers, many pubs are particularly walker (and cyclist) friendly. Several of our selected pubs have an area set aside where walkers can eat and drink without the need to remove muddy boots. Many pubs are centuries old, and you can't get more historic than The Bingley Arms, which claims the title of the oldest inhabited inn and brewhouse in England.

lesser known Wolds Way, which has a lot of archaeological interest. This book also contains a walk along part of the Leeds and Liverpool Canal, routes in the Yorkshire Dales National Park, a ride through the Dalby Forest and a circular walk linking the former mining towns of Ledsham and Fairburn. You can walk through countryside divided by the dry-stone walls typical of the Dales countryside, go past settlements once occupied by the Romans or cycle to York on the trackbed of the former King's Cross to Edinburgh railway line. For a coastal route, walk along the Cleveland Way, north of Robin Hood's Bay.

Dawn in the North York Moors National Park

Using this book

Each walk and cycle ride has a coloured panel giving essential information for the walker and cyclist, including the distance, terrain, nature of the paths, and where to park your car.

1			4
3h00	8.5 MILES	13.7 KM	LEVEL 1 2 3

SHORTER ALTERNATIVE ROUTE

1h30	4 MILES	6.4 KM	LEVEL 1 2 3

2 — **MAP:** OS Explorer OL24 White Peak

START/FINISH: Rudyard Old Station, grid ref
3 — SJ 955579

TRAILS/TRACKS: old railway trackbed

LANDSCAPE: wooded lake shore, peaceful pastures and meadows

PUBLIC TOILETS: Rudyard village

5 — **TOURIST INFORMATION:** Leek, tel 01538 483741

6 — **CYCLE HIRE:** none near by

THE PUB: The Abbey Inn, Leek, see Directions to the pub, page 27

7 — ❗ Take care along the banks of the lake – keep well away from the shore line

---

1 MINIMUM TIME: The time stated for completing each route is the estimated minimum time that a reasonably fit family group of walkers or cyclists would take to complete the circuit. This does not allow for rest or refreshment stops.

2 MAPS: Each route is shown on a detailed map. However, some detail is lost because of the restrictions imposed by scale, so for this reason, we recommend that you use the maps in conjunction with a more detailed Ordnance Survey map. The relevant Ordnance Survey Explorer map appropriate for each walk or cycle is listed.

3 START/FINISH: Here we indicate the start location and parking area. There is a six-figure grid reference prefixed by two letters showing which 100km square of the National Grid it refers to. You'll find more information on grid references on most Ordnance Survey maps.

4 LEVEL OF DIFFICULTY: The walks and cycle rides have been graded simply (1 to 3) to give an indication of their relative difficulty. Easier routes, such as those with little total ascent, on easy footpaths or level trails, or those covering shorter distances are graded 1. The hardest routes, either because they include a lot of ascent, greater distances, or are in hilly, more demanding terrains, are graded 3.

5 TOURIST INFORMATION: The nearest tourist information office and contact number is given for further local information, in particular opening details for the attractions listed in the 'Where to go from here' section.

6 CYCLE HIRE: We list, within reason, the nearest cycle hire shop/centre.

7 ❗ Here we highlight any potential difficulties or dangers along the route. At a glance you will know if the walk is steep or crosses difficult terrain, or if a cycle route is hilly, encounters a main road, or whether a mountain bike is essential for the off-road trails. If a particular route is suitable for older, fitter children we say so here.

About the pub

Generally, all the pubs featured are on the walk or cycle route. Some are close to the start/finish point, others are at the midway point, and occasionally, the recommended pub is a short drive from the start/finish point. We have included a cross-section of pubs, from homely village locals and isolated rural gems to traditional inns and upmarket country pubs which specialise in food. What they all have in common is that they serve food and welcome children.

The description of the pub is intended to convey its history and character and in the 'food' section we list a selection of dishes, which indicate the style of food available. Under 'family facilities', we say if the pub offers a children's menu or smaller portions of adult dishes, and whether the pub has a family room, highchairs, baby-changing facilities, or toys. There is detail on the garden, terrace, and any play area.

DIRECTIONS: If the pub is very close to the start point we state see Getting to the Start. If the pub is on the route the relevant direction/map location number is given, in addition to general directions. In some cases the pub is a short drive away from the finish point, so we give detailed directions to the pub from the end of the route.

PARKING: The number of parking spaces is given. All but a few of the walks and rides start away from the pub. If the pub car park is the parking/start point, then we have been given permission by the landlord to print the fact. You should always let the landlord or a member of staff know that you are using the car park before setting off.

OPEN: If the pub is open all week we state 'daily' and if it's open throughout the day we say 'all day', otherwise we just give the days/sessions the pub is closed.

FOOD: If the pub serves food all week we state 'daily' and if food is served throughout the day we say 'all day', otherwise we just give the days/sessions when food is not served.

BREWERY/COMPANY: This is the name of the brewery to which the pub is tied or the pub company that owns it. 'Free house' means that the pub is independently owned and run.

REAL ALE: We list the regular real ales available on handpump. 'Guest beers' indicates that the pub rotates beers from a number of microbreweries.

DOGS: We say if dogs are allowed in pubs on walk routes and detail any restrictions.

ROOMS: We list the number of bedrooms and how many are en suite. For prices please call the pub.

Please note that pubs change hands frequently and new chefs are employed, so menu details and facilities may change at short notice. Not all the pubs featured in this guide are listed in the *AA Pub Guide*. For information on those that are, including AA-rated accommodation, and for a comprehensive selection of pubs across Britain, please refer to the *AA Pub Guide* or see the AA's website www.theAA.com

Alternative refreshment stops

At a glance you will see if there are other pubs or cafés along the route. If there are no other places on the route, we list the nearest village or town where you can find somewhere else to eat and drink.

☛ Where to go from here

Many of the routes are short and may only take a few hours. You may wish to explore the surrounding area after lunch or before tackling the route, so we have selected a few attractions with children in mind.

Walking and cycling in safety

WALKING

All the walks are suitable for families, but less experienced family groups, especially those with younger children, should try the shorter or easier walks first. Route finding is usually straightforward, but the maps are for guidance only and we recommend that you always take the suggested Ordnance Survey map with you.

Risks

Although each walk has been researched with a view to minimising any risks, no walk in the countryside can be considered to be completely free from risk. Walking in the outdoors will always require a degree of common sense and judgement to ensure that it is as safe as possible, especially for young children.

- Be particularly careful on cliff paths and in upland terrain, where the consequences of a slip can be serious.
- Remember to check tidal conditions before walking on the seashore.
- Some sections of route are by, or cross, busy roads. Remember traffic is a danger even on minor country lanes.
- Be careful around farmyard machinery and livestock.
- Be aware of the consequences of changes in the weather and check the forecast before you set out. Ensure the whole family is properly equipped, wearing warm clothing and a good pair of boots or sturdy walking shoes. Take waterproof clothing with you and carry spare clothing and a torch if you are walking in the winter months. Remember the weather can change quickly at any time of the year, and in moorland and heathland areas, mist and fog can make route finding much harder. In summer, take account of the heat and sun by wearing a hat and carrying enough water.

- On walks away from centres of population you should carry a whistle and survival bag. If you do have an accident requiring emergency services, make a note of your position as accurately as possible and dial 999.

CYCLING

Cycling is a fun activity which children love, and teaching your child to ride a bike, and going on family cycling trips, are rewarding experiences. Not only is cycling a great way to travel, but as a regular form of exercise it can make an invaluable contribution to a child's health and fitness, and increase their confidence and sense of independence.

The growth of motor traffic has made Britain's roads increasingly dangerous and unattractive to cyclists. Cycling with children is an added responsibility and, as with everything, there is a risk when taking them out for a day's cycling. However, in recent years many measures have been taken to address this, including the on-going development of the National Cycle Network (8,000 miles utilising quiet lanes and traffic-free paths) and local designated off-road routes for families, such as converted railway lines, canal towpaths and forest tracks.

In devising the cycle rides in this guide, every effort has been made to use these designated cycle paths, or to link them with quiet country lanes and waymarked byways and bridleways. Unavoidably, in a few cases, some relatively busy B-roads have been used to link the quieter, more attractive routes.

Rules of the road

- Ride in single file on narrow and busy roads.
- Be alert, look and listen for traffic, especially on narrow lanes and blind bends and be extra careful when descending steep hills, as loose gravel can lead to an accident.
- In wet weather make sure you keep a good distance between you and other riders.
- Make sure you indicate your intentions clearly.
- Brush up on *The Highway Code* before venturing out on to the road.

Off-road safety code of conduct

- Only ride where you know it is legal to do so. It is forbidden to cycle on public footpaths, marked in yellow. The only 'rights of way' open to cyclists are bridleways (blue markers) and unsurfaced tracks, known as byways, which are open to all traffic and waymarked in red.
- Canal towpaths: you need a permit to cycle on some stretches of towpath (www.waterscape.com). Remember that access paths can be steep and slippery and always get off and push your bike under low bridges and by locks.

- Always yield to walkers and horses, giving adequate warning of your approach.
- Don't expect to cycle at high speeds.
- Keep to the main trail to avoid any unnecessary erosion to the area beside the trail and to prevent skidding, especially if it is wet.
- Remember the Country Code.

Cycling with children

Children can use a child seat from the age of eight months, or from the time they can hold themselves upright. There are a number of child seats available which fit on the front or rear of a bike and towable two-seat trailers are worth investigating. 'Trailer bicycles', suitable for five- to ten-year-olds, can be attached to the rear of an adult's bike, so that the adult has control, allowing the child to pedal if he/she wishes. Family cycling can be made easier by using a tandem, as it can carry a child seat and tow trailers. 'Kiddy-cranks' for shorter legs can be fitted to the rear seat tube, enabling either parent to take their child out cycling. With older children it is better to purchase the right size bike rather than one that is too big, as an oversized bike will be difficult to control, and potentially dangerous.

Preparing your bicycle

A basic routine includes checking the wheels for broken spokes or excess play in the bearings, and checking the tyres for punctures, undue wear and the correct tyre pressures. Ensure that the brake blocks are firmly in place and not worn, and that cables are not frayed or too slack. Lubricate hubs, pedals, gear mechanisms and cables. Make sure you have a pump, a bell, a rear rack to carry panniers and, if cycling at night, a set of working lights.

Preparing yourself

Equipping the family with cycling clothing need not be an expensive exercise. Comfort is the key when considering what to wear. Essential items for well-being on a bike are padded cycling shorts, warm stretch leggings (avoid tight-fitting and seamed trousers like jeans or baggy tracksuit trousers that may become caught in the chain), stiff-soled training shoes, and a wind and waterproof jacket. Fingerless gloves will add to your comfort.

A cycling helmet provides essential protection if you fall off your bike, so they are particularly recommended for young children learning to cycle.

Wrap your child up with several layers in colder weather. Make sure you and those with you are easily visible by car drivers and other road users, by wearing light-coloured or luminous clothing in daylight and reflective strips or sashes in failing light and when it is dark.

What to take with you

Invest in a pair of medium-sized panniers (rucksacks are unwieldy and can affect balance) to carry the necessary gear for you and your family for the day. Take extra clothes with you, the amount depending on the season, and always pack a light wind/waterproof jacket. Carry a basic tool kit (tyre levers, adjustable spanner, a small screwdriver, puncture repair kit, a set of Allen keys) and practical spares, such as an inner tube, a universal brake/gear cable, and a selection of nuts and bolts. Also, always take a pump and a strong lock.

Cycling, especially in hilly terrain and off-road, saps energy, so take enough food and drink for your outing. Always carry plenty of water, especially in hot and humid weather conditions. Consume high-energy snacks like cereal bars, cake or fruits, eating little and often to combat feeling weak and tired. Remember that children get thirsty (and hungry) much more quickly than adults so always have food and diluted juices available for them.

And finally, the most important advice of all—enjoy yourselves!

USEFUL CYCLING WEBSITES

NATIONAL CYCLE NETWORK
A comprehensive network of safe and attractive cycle routes throughout the UK.
It is co-ordinated by the route construction charity Sustrans with the support of more than 450 local authorities and partners across Britain. For maps, leaflets and more information on the designated off-road cycle trails across the country contact
www.sustrans.org.uk
www.nationalcyclenetwork.org.uk

LONDON CYCLING CAMPAIGN
Pressure group that lobbies MPs, organises campaigns and petitions in order to improve cycling conditions in the capital. It provides maps, leaflets and information on cycle routes across London.
www.lcc.org.uk

BRITISH WATERWAYS
For information on towpath cycling, visit
www.waterscape.com

FORESTRY COMMISSION
For information on cycling in Forestry Commission woodland see
www.forestry.gov.uk/recreation

CYCLISTS TOURING CLUB
The largest cycling club in Britain, provides information on cycle touring, and legal and technical matters
www.ctc.org.uk

From Austwick to Wharfe

WALK

From Austwick along ancient tracks to see the famous Norber Erratics.

Austwick

A pleasant, grey-built village, Austwick has several old cottages, many of them dated in the traditional Dales way by a decorative lintel above the main door, showing the initials of the couple who built it and the year they moved in.

The walk takes you up Town Head Lane from the village, and across fields into Thwaite Lane. To your left is the ridge of limestone called Robin Proctor's Scar, named after a local farmer whose horse was trained to bring him home after a long night spent in the local pub. One night, too drunk to tell, he mounted the wrong horse, and it plunged over the crag with the farmer on its back. The area below the scar was formerly a tarn, and is now home to a wide variety of marsh plants. Nappa Scar, which

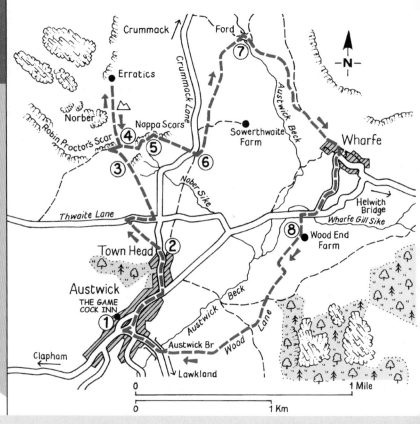

Austwick

NORTH YORKSHIRE

A walker crossing a clapper bridge in Crummackdale

2h30 — 5.5 **MILES** — 8.8 **KM** — **LEVEL 2**

MAP: OS Explorer OL2 Yorkshire Dales – Southern & Western

START/FINISH: roadside parking in Austwick village; grid ref: SD 767684

PATHS: field and moorland paths tracks, lanes on return, 10 stiles

LANDSCAPE: farmland and limestone upland

PUBLIC TOILETS: none on route

TOURIST INFORMATION: Settle, tel 01729 825192

THE PUB: The Game Cock, Austwick

the walk passes after you have visited the Norber Erratics, is on the North Craven Fault line. The path goes along a ledge below a steep cliff and the cliff wall has different strata of rock, including mixed conglomerate and limestone.

The Norber Erratics are world famous. To geologists they are a place of pilgrimage, and even the non-specialist can tell that something odd is going on here. When you arrive on the plateau above Nappa Scar, you find an extensive grass-covered area, with the remnants of a limestone pavement poking through the tufts. Strewn all over the pavement are grey boulders, some of them huge, perched on limestone plinths. These are the Erratics. Blocks of ancient greywacke stone, they were carried here from nearby Crummackdale by the power of a glacier, and dumped when the ice retreated. Over time the elements have worn down the limestone pavement on which they stand – except where the erratics protected it, resulting in their elevated position.

The Norber Arratics – ancient greywacke stone – were delivered here by an Ice Age glacier

Getting to the start

Austwick lies beneath the Ingleborough massif's limestone scars, just 1 mile (1.6km) north off the A65 road and 6 miles (9.7km) northwest of Settle. There's no formal car park, but there's a limited amount of roadside parking by the green. Arrive early if you're visiting at the weekend.

Researched and written by:
John Gillham, David Winpenny

the walk

1 From the Game Cock Inn and the triangular green in the centre of the Austwick village, walk northwards out of the village, following the signpost to Horton in Ribblesdale. Pass the Game Cock Inn and, just past a cottage called Hob's Gate, turn left up **Town Head Lane**. Just after the road bends round to the right, go left over a waymarked ladder stile.

2 Walk through the field to another stile, and on to another stile on to a lane. Turn right. Just before reaching a metalled road, turn left over a ladder stile and follow the line of the track. As the track veers left, go straight on, following the line of the stone wall to a stone stile by a gate.

3 Go through the gate and continue along the rocky track. Where the stone wall on your left bends left, by a very large boulder across the path, go right on a track to pass the right-hand edge of the scar. When you reach a signpost, go left, signposted '**Norber**'.

4 Follow the path uphill, to the plateau, and explore the **Norber Erratics**. Return the same way, back to the signpost. Turn left, following the sign to **Crummack**. Follow the track as it winds downhill then up beside a wall by the scar to a stone stile on your right.

5 Descend to another stile and follow the path beneath a rocky outcrop, which goes downhill with a wall to the left to reach a ladder stile on to a metalled lane. Cross the lane and go over another ladder stile opposite.

6 Turn left across the field. Go over two ladder stiles, cross a tarred lane and go over a ridge of rock to a stone stile then a ladder stile. Go over the stile and left to reach a track. Turn right and cross the **ford** on a clapper bridge.

7 Follow the track between the walls for 0.5 mile (800m) into **Wharfe**. Turn left by the bridleway sign in the village, then follow the road round to the right and go down the village approach road to reach a metalled road. Turn right. After 100yds (91m) turn left at a bridleway sign to Wood Lane, down the road to **Wood End Farm**.

8 By the farm buildings the track goes right. Follow it as it bends left and right to a crossroads of tracks. Go straight ahead, following the line of **telegraph poles**. The track winds to reach the metalled lane into the village. Turn right over the bridge to the village centre.

what to look for

Nothing is as characteristic of the Yorkshire Dales as its limestone scenery. It is technically known to geologists as a karst landscape – one that has underground drainage, with sinkholes and caves, dry valleys and limestone pavements like the one above Austwick. Unlike most rocks, limestone is a soluble stone that is constantly being cleaned by the action of rainfall. Soils are not formed, plants do not appear, and the limestone remains pristine in its whiteness. But it is certainly not an unchanging landscape. The glaciers which originally scraped clean the limestone pavements have left their mark elsewhere, in the deep-gouged valleys and in the clefts in the landscape where their melt waters have torn through the rock. Even more spectacular are the caves under your feet, and the mysterious entrances to them. As you walk through this landscape, stalagmites and stalactites are still being formed beneath your feet.

The Game Cock

In the Three Peaks area north of Settle in a pretty limestone village, this is a cosy family-run pub popular with locals. Inside, you'll find a homely wood-floored bar with built-in wall benches, hand-pulled Thwaites Bitter, pub games and an open fire, a more formal carpeted restaurant and a light and airy conservatory dining area. There are tables and parasols looking across to the village green, and to the rear is a lawned area for alfresco dining.

Food
Sandwiches (Angus beef) and snacks like Thai green chicken curry and scampi and chips are served only in the bar. Off the main menu, start with a crab and saffron tartlet or black pudding with mustard sauce, then move on to game-cock pie, lamb shoulder with minted jus or freshly battered haddock. Finish with white chocolate and Bailey's cheesecake.

Family facilities
The good play area and aviaries in the rear garden will keep children amused on fine days and they are welcome inside, where small portions of adult meals are available as well as a children's menu and high chairs.

about the pub

The Game Cock
The Green, Austwick
Settle, North Yorkshire LA2 8BB
Tel: 01524 251226
www.lordsinns.co.uk

DIRECTIONS: see Getting to the Start; pub by the village green	
PARKING: 5	
OPEN: daily; all day Sunday and all day Saturday from Easter to September	
FOOD: daily; all day Sunday	
BREWERY/COMPANY: Thwaites Brewery	
REAL ALE: Thwaites Best	
DOGS: welcome inside after food hours and in the garden	
ROOMS: 5 bedrooms	

Alternative refreshment stops
On the A65 just outside the village is the Cross Streets Inn. The Austwick Country House Hotel offers morning coffee, afternoon teas, bar lunches, sandwiches and an extensive restaurant menu.

☛ Where to go from here
Clapham village has a beck flowing through its centre, and is surrounded by attractive woodland. Take a guided tour of Ingleborough Cave to view magnificent limestone formations set in large, lit passages, or visit Settle's Museum of North Craven Life.

Hawes and Hardraw

WALK

From busy Hawes to Hardraw, with a visit to the famous waterfall.

Hawes & Hardraw

NORTH YORKSHIRE

Hardraw Force

For many people, Hawes means two things – Wensleydale cheese and motorcyclists. The bikers use the town as a base at summer weekends and bank holidays, enjoying a friendly drink in the pubs and spectacular rides on the surrounding roads. However, it is the Wensleydale Creamery that attracts other visitors. Just above the car park in Gayle Lane, the Creamery offers tours and tastings, as well as the chance to buy a traditional Wensleydale.

Cheese has been made in Wensleydale since French monks brought the skill here in 1150. After centuries of farm production, a factory was started in Hawes in 1897. It was saved from closure in the 1930s by local man Kit Calvert, and again in 1992, when the local managers bought the creamery from Dairy Crest. It is now a thriving business and a vital part of the Hawes economy.

The walk gives you the chance – which you should take – to visit the famous Hardraw Force, a 90ft (27m) waterfall in a deep and narrow valley. There is a modest entrance charge, payable in The Green Dragon Inn in Hardraw village, and a short, pleasant walk to the fall. Despite appearances, what you see isn't entirely natural. On 12 July 1889 an unprecedented deluge on the hill above caused a wall of water to descend Hardraw Beck and through the valley, destroying buildings in the village and washing away bridges. It also devastated the waterfall, reducing it

to a mudslide. After seeing to the clearing up in the village and the welfare of his tenants, the local landowner, Lord Wharncliffe, arranged for his workmen to reconstruct the lip of the fall, pinning together the blocks of shattered stone. This he did so successfully that today's visitors have no idea of the disaster that happened more than a century ago.

the walk

1 From the top end of the car park turn left, then go right over a stile signed 'Youth Hostel'. The path flirts with a track, which soon ends by a **stone outbuilding**, then climbs uphill to a stile. Continue west across several fields passing a barn and crossing a lane, to reach the B road. Turn left, then right through a gate signed **'Thorney Mire House'**. Follow the path for 0.5 mile (800m) to a gate on to a lane. Turn right. Follow this for 0.75 mile (1.2km), passing under the viaduct to the road at **Appersett**.

The spectacular waterfall of Hardraw Force in the Yorkshire Dales National Park

2h30 — **6 MILES** — **9.7 KM** — **LEVEL 1 2 3**

MAP: OS Explorer OL30 Yorkshire Dales – Northern & Central

START/FINISH: pay car park off Gayle Lane at west side of Hawes; grid ref: SD 870898

PATHS: field and moorland paths, may be muddy, 44 stiles

LANDSCAPE: moorland and farmland

PUBLIC TOILETS: at car park

TOURIST INFORMATION: Hawes, tel 01969 667450

THE PUB: The Green Dragon Inn, Hardraw

❗ Take care on bustling Hawes streets

Getting to the start

Hawes is on the main A684 road, which links the M6 near Sedbergh with the A1 near Northallerton. This bustling market town has two car parks. The one used here is at the west side of the town, just off the minor road to Gayle.

Researched and written by:
John Gillham, David Winpenny

2 Turn left across the bridge. Follow the road and cross the next bridge, then bend left to the junction. Go through a stile, signed **'Bluebell Hill'**. Cross the field, go through a gate and over a bridge, then bear half left uphill. Go through a gate and continue to a crossroads signpost.

3 Turn right and follow the valley to a stile (**Bob's Stile**). Cross the field beyond, go over a stile, then turn left to a ladder stile over a wall. Cross the field towards Hardraw, going over a wooden stile, then over a ladder stile into a lane.

4 Turn right, then left at the main road and cross the bridge. Hardraw Force entrance is through **The Green Dragon Inn**, so you can see it before or after refreshment. Immediately beyond the pub, turn left and go right through a signed gate in the wall, through a courtyard and over a stile. Follow the flagged path over another stile, steeply uphill, over a stile and up steps. By the house, go through a stile and right of the

what to look for

Redshank and widgeon are among the birds that you may see on the walk, especially around the pond by the New Bridge near Appersett (the second one you cross here). The wading redshank, with its long legs, has a characteristic alarm call and nests in grass, laying four eggs during the breeding season from April to July. Look out for the characteristic white bar across its wings. Widgeon, members of the duck family, graze on wet meadowland, often in huge flocks. The male has a rusty-red head with an orange crown, while the female is plainer, though of a distinctive dull orange colour.

stables, then through two more stiles on to a lane by the **Simonstone Hall Hotel**.

5 Turn right, then left along the road. Almost immediately turn right through a stile signed '**Sedbusk**'. Follow the track through a metal gate and over two ladder

stiles and another gateway, then through 14 stiles into Sedbusk.

6 Turn right along the road, bend left near the post-box and go downhill. Go right, over a stile signed '**Haylands Bridge**'. Cross the field, bend right to a stile in a crossing wall, then down to a stile on to a road. Cross to another stile and follow the path, cross a stream, go over a stile, then bear right over a humpback bridge. Go through a gated stile on to a road.

7 Turn left. Cross Haylands Bridge and beyond go right through a kissing gate signed '**Hawes**'. Follow the path, go over a stile, then turn left, then right on to the main road. At the junction cross and turn right past the post office. Follow the main road through Hawes, turning left after the school to the car park.

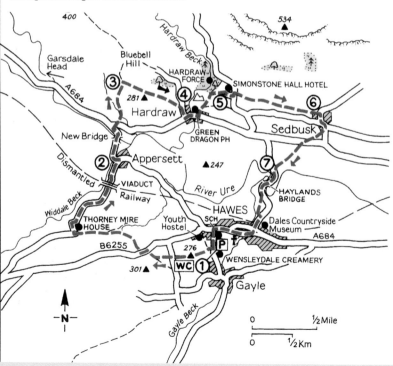

The Green Dragon Inn

The Green Dragon is a legendary old Dales pub with a history dating back to the 16th century when it was an outpost for Cistercian monks from Jervaulx Abbey. Today, it's a great walkers' pub, with its own footpath to Hardraw Force, England's highest unbroken waterfall, beginning from its back door. Little has changed inside over the years, with a big panelled public bar and a cosy, beamed snug bar with a glowing coal fire in a fine old range, traditional benches, tables and chairs, and cracking real ales from Yorkshire micro-breweries on hand-pump. Lovely rear garden and 15 acres (6ha) of woodland with superb views.

Expect a warm welcome and, if you're lucky, you may arrive when the Hardraw Gathering (Folk Festival) is in full swing.

Food
Food is hearty and traditional pub fare. The popular menu takes in filled baguettes, gammon and egg, lasagne and good home-made dishes like game casserole, rabbit pie, pheasant in red wine and chicken and leek pie, with vegetarian options. Home-made apple pie for pudding.

Family facilities
Children are very welcome inside. The pub has a family room and a large garden.

Alternative refreshment stops
There is plenty of choice in Hawes with its pubs, cafés and tea rooms, as well as a fish and chip shop. More upmarket is the Simonstone Hall Hotel, on the walk between Hardraw and Sedbusk.

☛ Where to go from here
To find out more about life in the Dales, visit the Dales Countryside Museum (www.destinationdales.org) in the Station Yard at Hawes. Here you can walk through a Time Tunnel that takes you back through 10,000 years of Dales' history, and see how life has changed over the centuries. Also included in the admission charge is a trip 'down' a lead mine, a visit to an old doctor's surgery, and the nostalgia of a kitchen in the Dales from the last century.

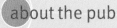

about the pub

The Green Dragon Inn
Hardraw, Hawes
North Yorkshire DL8 3LZ
Tel: 01969 667392
www.greendragonhardraw.com

DIRECTIONS:	Hardraw is signposted north off the A684 in Hawes. Pub is beside the river bridge
PARKING:	50
OPEN:	daily; all day
FOOD:	daily; all day
BREWERY/COMPANY:	free house
REAL ALE:	Theakston Bitter & Old Peculier, Black Sheep Bitter, Timothy Taylor Landlord, York Bitter, guest beers
DOGS:	allowed in bars and garden
ROOMS:	17 en suite

From Keld to Muker

A classic walk in Upper Swaledale from Keld to Muker along Kisdon Side, and back by the river.

Keld and Muker

Keld – its name is the Old Norse word for a spring – is one of the most remote of Dales villages. Set at the head of Swaledale, its cluster of grey cottages is a centre for some of the most spectacular walks in North Yorkshire. This walk follows, for part of its way, the traditional route by which the dead of the upper Dales were taken the long distance for burial in Grinton churchyard. Leaving the village, the walk takes the Pennine Way as it follows the sweep of the Swale on its way down to Muker. This is Kisdon Side, on the slopes of the conical hill known as Kisdon. It was formed at the end of the Ice Age; the Swale used to flow west of the hill but glacial debris blocked its course and forced it to the east, in its current bed.

As the Pennine Way goes west, eventually to climb the slopes of Great Shunner Fell, the walk joins the Corpse Way and descends into Muker. It is worth taking some time to explore the village. Like many Swaledale settlements, it expanded in the 18th and 19th centuries because of local lead-mining. The prominent Literary Institute was built for the mining community; though in a nice reverse of fortunes, when the new chapel came to be built in the 1930s, dressed stone taken from the ore hearths at the Old Gang Mine down the valley was used. The Anglican church, which eventually did away with the long journey to Grinton, dates from 1580.

Beyond Muker, the walk passes through hay meadows and along the banks of the Swale. Both sandstone and limestone are found in this section; look out for the sandstone bed underlying the river. The limestone of the area is part of the thick Ten Fathom bed, one of the Yoredale series of sedimentary rocks. Where the valley of Swinner Gill crosses the path are the remains of a small smelt mill which served the nearby Beldi Hill and Swinner Gill Mines.

Top: traditional hay meadows in fields near Muker in the Yorkshire Dales National Park

As you ascend the hill beyond, the ruins of Crackpot Hall, a farmhouse long abandoned because of mining subsidence and changes in farming fortune, are to your right. Its name means 'Crows Pothole'.

the walk

1 Walk back down the car park entrance road, and straight ahead down the gravel track, signed **'Muker'**. Continue along at the upper level, ignoring a path downhill to the left. Go through a gate, ignoring the left fork path signed to Kisdon Upper Force.

2 At another signpost take the right fork – the **Pennine Way** route. The narrow path traverses rough stony hillsides high above the Swale before easing down bracken-covered sheep pastures towards Muker.

Below: a view across Swaledale of green fields divided by small stone walls on the Pennine Way

WALK

2h30 — **6 MILES** — **9.7 KM** — **LEVEL 1 2 3**

MAP: Explorer OL30 Yorkshire Dales – Northern & Central

START/FINISH: signed car park at west end of Keld near Park Lodge; grid ref: NY 892012

PATHS: field and riverside paths and tracks, 10 stiles

LANDSCAPE: hillside and valley, hay meadows, riverside and waterfall

PUBLIC TOILETS: Keld and Muker

TOURIST INFORMATION: Reeth, tel 01748 884059

THE PUB: The Farmers Arms, Muker

Getting to the start

Keld sleeps high on pastured hills, right at the end of Swaledale. It's on the B6270 road 9 miles (14.5km) from Kirkby Stephen and 20 miles (32km) from Richmond. There is a good car park at the west end of the village.

Researched and written by:
John Gillham, David Winpenny

Keld   **NORTH YORKSHIRE**

3 Where the Pennine Way goes right, leave it to follow a walled path signed 'Muker'. This joins a stony farm track, which winds down to the north end of the village.

4 Those who wish to visit The Farmers Arms should follow the lane all the way to the main Swaledale road. Otherwise, turn left and left again by a sign to **Gunnerside** and **Keld**. Follow the paved path across hay fields to reach the river. Turn right and go over a stile to the footbridge.

5 Ascend the steps beyond the footbridge and turn left to join a stony track, signed '**Keld**'. This follows the course of the river before crossing a tributary, **Swinner Gill**, on a footbridge by some old lead mine workings.

6 The track climbs the hill and into woodland before being joined by Wainwright's Coast-to-Coast track beneath Crackpot Hall.

7 Go left by a wooden seat, at a sign to Keld. Follow the stream by **East Gill Force** waterfalls down to a footbridge. Go through the gate and turn right, uphill, to a T-junction, where you turn right and follow the path back to the car.

what to look for

Around Muker traditional hay meadows are still to be found. They are an important part of the farmer's regime, which is why signs ask you to keep to single file as you walk through them. Such a method of farming helps maintain the wide variety of wild flowers that grow in the hay meadows. The barns, too, are part of older farming patterns, and form one of the most important visual assets of the Dales. The Muker area is especially rich in them – there are 60 within half a mile (800m) of the village. Their purpose was to store the hay after it was cut, to feed the three or four animals that would be over-wintered inside. This was to save the farmer moving stock and hauling loads of hay long distances. It also meant that the manure from the beasts could be used on the field just outside the barn.

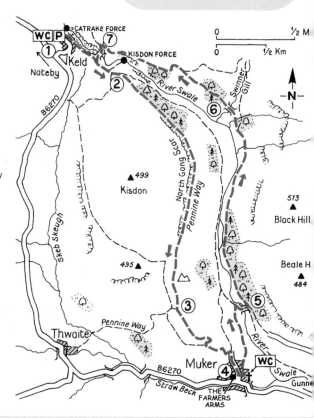

The Farmers Arms

In a raised position at the centre of the village, the 17th-century whitewashed Farmers Arms is a simple Dales pub at the head of beautiful Swaledale, popular with walkers on the Pennine Way and the Coast-to-Coast route. Take a seat by the fire in the main bar and sup a pint of Theakston in unspoilt surroundings – flagstone floors, old pine settles, heavy beams and plenty of plates and tankards on display. Outside on the terrace there are views of the village and across the green valley of the Swale to the hillsides beyond.

Food

Hearty traditional food at good prices is popular with local farmers and famished walkers. Tuck into bacon baps, cheese and onion toasties, filled jacket potatoes and specials like beef in Guinness and fish pie at lunchtime. Evening additions include pasta with chicken and a tomato and herb sauce, liver and onions, shank of lamb, and steaks with home-made sauces.

Family facilities

Children are very welcome inside the pub. Younger family members have their own menu and portions of adult dishes are served. High chairs and small cutlery are also available.

Alternative refreshment stops

Park Lodge in Keld provides tea, coffee and light refreshments, and so does the Village Store in Muker.

☞ Where to go from here

Take the minor road that leaves the B6270 just west of Keld to reach Tan Hill and its inn, the highest in England at 1,732 feet (528m) above sea level. Learn more about the history and culture of Swaledale during a visit to the Swaledale Folk Museum in Reeth, or to the Old Working Smithy and Museum at nearby Gunnerside.

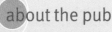

about the pub

The Farmers Arms
Muker, Richmond
North Yorkshire DL11 6QG
Tel: 01748 886297

DIRECTIONS: village centre beside the B6270	
PARKING: 6	
OPEN: daily; all day	
FOOD: daily	
BREWERY/COMPANY: free house	
REAL ALE: Black Sheep Best, Theakston Best and Old Peculier, John Smith's Cask, Camerons Nimmo's XXXX	
DOGS: welcome inside	

Along Langstrothdale from Hubberholme

Hubberholme

From J B Priestley's favourite Dales village, along Langstrothdale and back via a limestone terrace.

Hubberholme and Langstrothdale

Literary pilgrims visit Hubberholme to see The George Inn, where J B Priestley could often be found enjoying the local ale, and the churchyard, the last resting place for his ashes, as he requested. He chose an idyllic spot. Set at the foot of Langstrothdale, Hubberholme is a cluster of old farmhouses and cottages surrounding the church. Norman in origin, St Michael's was once flooded so badly that fish were seen swimming in the nave. One vicar of Hubberholme is said to have carelessly baptised a child Amorous instead of Ambrose, a mistake that, once entered in the parish register, couldn't be altered. Amorous Stanley used his memorable name later in life as part of his stock-in-trade as a hawker.

Hubberholme church's best treasures are of wood. The rood loft above the screen is one of only two surviving in Yorkshire, (the other is at Flamborough, far away on the east coast). Master-carver Robert Thompson provided almost all the rest of the furniture in 1934 – look for his mouse trademark on each piece.

Yockenthwaite's name, said to have been derived from an ancient Irish name, Eogan, conjures up images of the ancient past. Norse settlers were here more than 1,000 years ago – and even earlier settlers have left their mark, a Bronze Age stone circle a little further up the valley. The hamlet now consists of a few farm buildings beside the bridge over the Wharfe at the end of Langstrothdale Chase, a Norman hunting ground which once had its own forest laws and punishments. You walk along a typical Dales limestone terrace to reach Cray, on the road over from Bishopdale joining Wharfedale to Wensleydale. Here is another huddle of farmhouses, around the White Lion Inn.

You then follow the Cray Gill downstream, past a series of small cascades. For a more spectacular waterfall, head up the road a little way to Cray High Bridge.

Back in Hubberholme, the George Inn was once the vicarage and each New Year's Day is the scene of an ancient auction. It begins with the lighting of a candle, after which the auctioneer asks for bids for the year's tenancy of the 'Poor Pasture', a 16 acre (6.5ha) field behind the inn. All bids must be completed before the candle burns out.

The interior of St Michael's church in the Yorkshire Dales

The Mouse Man's signature from Hubberholme's 15th-century Church of St Michael

the walk

1 Go through a Dales Way signed gate near the east end of the church, bend left and then take the lower path, signed 'Yockenthwaite'. Walk beside the **river** for 1.75 miles (2.8km) through three stiles, a gate and two more stiles. The path eventually rises to another stone stile into **Yockenthwaite**.

2 Go through the stile and bend left to a wooden gate. Continue through a farm gate by a sign to Deepdale and Beckermonds. Before the track reaches a bridge go right and swing round to a sign to **Cray**.

3 Go up the hill and, as the track curves right, continue it to follow a slightly higher grass track highlighted by a **Cray and Hubberholme sign**. Part-way up the hill go right at a footpath sign through a wooden gate in a fence.

4 Go through a second gate to a footpath sign and ascend the hillside. Go through a gap in a wall by another signpost and follow the obvious path through several gaps in crossing walls. The path climbs left to reach a stile at the edge of **woodland**.

5 Cross the bridge beyond and continue through the woodland, back on to high pasture. The high path follows a line of limestone crags with Buckden in the valley below before arcing left into the hollow of **Crook Gill**. Go over a footbridge spanning

MAP: OS Explorer OL30 Yorkshire Dales – Northern & Central

START/FINISH: Beside river in Hubberholme, opposite church (not church parking); grid ref: SD 927782

PATHS: field paths and tracks, steep after Yockenthwaite, 11 stiles

LANDSCAPE: streamside paths and limestone terrace

PUBLIC TOILETS: none on route

TOURIST INFORMATION: Grassington, tel 01756 752774

THE PUB: The George Inn, Hubberholme

Getting to the start

The tiny village of Hubberholme is situated in Upper Wharfedale 18 miles (29km) north of Skipton. From the A59 Skipton bypass, follow the B6160 north. In Buckden turn off left along a narrow country lane for Hubberholme. Cross the bridge by the George Inn, where there is roadside parking by the river.

Researched and written by:
John Gillham, David Winpenny

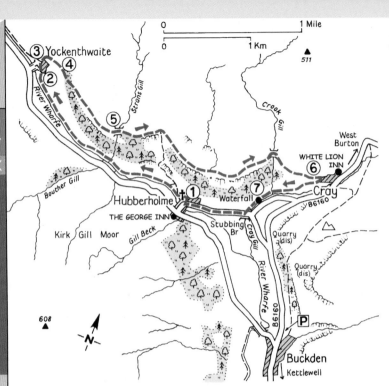

what to look for

A number of barns in the area have been converted to become holiday accommodation bunk barns. An initiative set up by the Yorkshire Dales National Park Authority and the Countryside Commission in 1979, the aim is to solve two problems – how to preserve the now-redundant barns that are so vital a part of the Dales landscape, and a lack of simple accommodation for walkers. Also known as stone tents, these bunkhouse barns offer farmers an alternative to letting the barns decay. They add basic amenities for cooking, washing and sleeping (and sometimes extras like comfortable chairs!) and let them to families or groups at a realistic nightly rate. They help to keep the farms viable, and both walkers and farmers benefit in other ways, too; meeting each other helps each to appreciate the needs and hopes of the other. As one farmer's wife said, 'We've made a lot of friends though the barn'.

the gill, then climb the far banks to pass to the right of a barn. The footpath winds its way down the valley side. Go through a gate and straight ahead across meadowland to a gateway on to a track, and on to a **stone barn**.

6 Bend to the right beyond the barn, down to a public footpath sign to **Stubbing Bridge**. Go down the path between stone walls and through a wooden gate and on to the grassy hillside. Continue downhill to meet the stream by a **waterfall**.

7 Continue along the streamside path through woodland. Go over a wooden stile and on past a barn to a stone stile on to the road. Turn right along the road back to the parking place in **Hubberholme**.

The George Inn

Ruggedly beautiful countryside, much loved by walkers, surrounds The George, a rough whitewashed stone building formerly owned by the church opposite and dating from 1600. It stands in a wonderfully peaceful setting on the banks of the Wharfe. Inside, it's a haven of unspoilt character, with splendid flagstone floors, thick, stripped stone walls, blackened beams and mullioned windows featuring throughout the homely bars. An open kitchen-range fireplace adds warmth in inclement weather, and a candle burns continuously on the bar, a reminder of the annual letting of the Poor Pasture. Sheltered patio for summer drinking.

Food

Home-cooked meals are prepared from local produce, with sandwiches, quiche, gammon, egg and chips and beefburgers served at lunchtimes. Evening dishes include Black Sheep casserole, Dales lamb chops with red wine gravy and steak and ale pie.

Family facilities

Children are welcome in part of the bar and youngsters have a standard menu to choose from. No under-14s overnight.

about the pub

The George Inn
Kirk Gill, Hubberholme
Skipton, North Yorkshire BD23 5JE
Tel: 01756 760223
www.thegeorge-inn.co.uk

DIRECTIONS: see Getting to the Start; pub opposite the bridge and lane leading to the church

PARKING: 20

OPEN: daily; closed one weekday November to Easter

FOOD: daily

BREWERY/COMPANY: free house

REAL ALE: Black Sheep Bitter, Copper Dragon Beers

DOGS: welcome in the garden only

ROOMS: 6 en suite

Alternative refreshment stops

The White Lion at Cray – slightly off the route – is worth a detour.

☞ Where to go from here

Head for Malham Cove to experience and explore some magnificent limestone scenery. Near Grassington at Greenhow is the Stump Cross Cavern, a 500-year-old cave with a superb collection of stalactites and stalagmites. Visit Parcevall Hall Gardens near Applewick (www.parcevallhallgardens.co.uk).

A circuit taking in Malham Cove

The noble Malham Cove is the majestic highlight of this quintessential limestone Dales walk.

Malham Water Sinks and Cove

As you begin this walk, the stream from Malham Tarn suddenly disappears in a tumble of rocks. This is the aptly named Water Sinks. In spectacular limestone country like this, it is not unusual for streams to plunge underground – it was subterranean watercourses that sculpted the cave systems beneath your feet. You will see as you continue that this particular

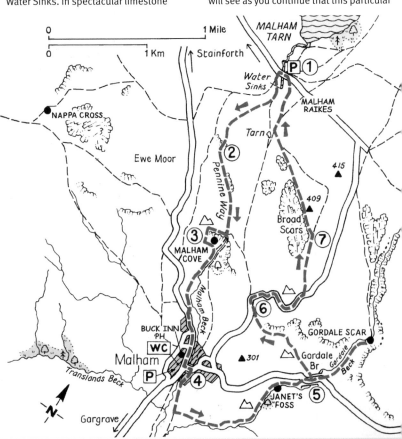

stream has not always been so secretive. The now-dry valley of Watlowes just beyond Water Sinks was formed by water action. It was this stream, in fact, that produced Malham Cove, and once fell over its spectacular cliff in a waterfall 230ft (70m) high. Although in very wet weather the stream goes a little further than Water Sinks, it is 200 years since water reached the cove.

Beyond Watlowes valley you reach a stretch of limestone pavement – not the biggest, but probably the best-known example of this unusual phenomenon in the Dales. The natural fissures in the rock have been enlarged by millennia of rain and frost, forming the characteristic blocks, called clints, and the deep clefts, called grikes.

the walk

1 From the car parking space, walk right along the lane and through the gate, before turning left through a kissing gate at the **Malham Raikes**, Langscar Gate sign. Walk down to the dry-stone wall on your left and follow a deepening dry valley. Beyond a cave in crags to the left, an engineered path doubles back right into a second dry valley.

2 Turn left and follow the footpath down the valley to reach the limestone pavement at the top of **Malham Cove**. Turn right and walk along the pavement to reach steps, which begin by an opening in a wall. Over 400 steps descend in zig-zags to the foot of the Cove.

3 When you reach the bottom, turn right along the path beside the river to reach

| 3h00 | 6.25 MILES | 10.1 KM | LEVEL 2 |

MAP: OS Explorer OL30 Yorkshire Dales – Northern & Central

START/FINISH: At Water Sinks, Malham Tarn, near gateway across road; grid ref: SD 894658

PATHS: well-marked field and moorland paths, more than 400 steps in descent from Malham Cove, 5 stiles

LANDSCAPE: spectacular limestone country, including Malham Cove

PUBLIC TOILETS: car park in Malham village

TOURIST INFORMATION: Malham, tel 01729 830363

THE PUB: The Buck Inn, Malham

🛈 Some slippery sections on the limestone in the dry valley preceding Malham Cove. Steep drops from Cove's edge

Getting to the start

Malham nestles at the head of the Aire Valley, 8 miles (13km) east of Settle. It is accessed by narrow lanes from Settle and from the A65 Leeds to Kendal road, between Gargrave and Hellifield. Drive through the village on the Malham Cove road, then turn right at the crossroads. The car park and start of the walk are on the left side of the road immediately south of Malham Tarn.

Researched and written by:
John Gillham, David Winpenny

Top: the New Bridge crossing Malham Beck is also known as the Monk's Bridge

the road. Turn left and follow the road into the centre of **Malham** village.

4 **The Buck Inn** lies on the right side of the road, just beyond the little bridge. Go over the bridge, then turn right along an unsurfaced lane between the river and a row of cottages. At the end a gravelled footpath signed 'Janet's Foss' heads south across fields. At a junction with the Pennine Way, turn left across more fields, then into woodland. At **Janet's Foss** the path climbs left to the Goredale road. Turn right along the road, towards **Gordale Scar**.

5 At the bridge go through a gate to the left. (To visit Gordale Scar, continue straight ahead here. Take a signed gate to the left and follow the path up through a field into the gorge. Keep going on the obvious route as far as the **waterfall,** then follow the same route back to the previously mentioned bridge.) On the main route, follow the signed public footpath uphill through two stiles and out on to a lane.

6 Turn right and walk uphill on the winding lane for 0.25 mile (400m), to a ladder stile over the wall on your left. Follow the track, going left at a fork to reach another **footpath fingerpost**.

7 Turn left along the edge of the limestone clints of **Broad Scars** to reach some **small pools**. Turn right at the sign for Malham Tarn, go over a ladder stile in a cross-wall, then take the left fork path and follow it back to the car park.

The path that leads to the natural amphitheatre at Malham Cove

what to look for

Nothing is what is seems in the Alice-in-Wonderland world around Malham. The logical among us would assume that if water disappears underground, heading in the direction of Malham Cove, just a mile (1.6km) ahead, it will reappear at the base of the Cove. But logic is wrong. The stream that bubbles up from under Malham Cove actually comes from Smelt Mill Sink, 0.75 mile (1.2km) to the west of Water Sinks. The stream from Water Sinks, on the other hand, reappears at Aire Head Springs to become the infant River Aire. All this is known from experiments first undertaken at the end of the 19th century and still continuing today. Several methods are used. One involves creating surges of water by opening and closing the sluice gates at the stream's exit from Malham Tarn. A more modern method dyes club-moss that can be collected in plankton nets and scanned with a fluorometer.

The Buck Inn

A rather grand hall-like stone building with mullioned windows, The Buck Inn was built in 1874 and is set in the heart of the village, near to the village green and the little packhorse bridge over the Aire (just a stream hereabouts). You can eat in style in the elegant restaurant and in the open-plan, carpeted lounge bar, or in the Hikers Bar, a simply furnished flag-floored room with scrubbed tables and local Copper Dragon beers on tap – perfect for booted walkers. There are benches outside for those who just want to watch the ducks glide along the nearby stream.

Food
An extensive menu lists a wide range of home-made pub food. For a snack there are filled baguettes (home-cooked ham and mustard mayonnaise) and jacket potatoes filled with chilli or cheese. For something more substantial there's home-battered fresh haddock and chips, pork and leek sausages, leek and macaroni cheese, and the famous Malham & Masham pie (beef and Old Peculier ale).

Family facilities
Children are welcome in the pub and there's a separate menu for younger family members. Pool table in the Hikers Bar.

Alternative refreshment stops
As one of the most visited villages of the Yorkshire Dales, Malham is well supplied with eating places. The Malham Café offers meals and snacks, while the Lister Arms Hotel provides good food, real ale and, in summer, real cider.

☛ Where to go from here
Head for Settle and enjoy a ride on the Carlisle to Settle Railway (www.settle-carlisle.co.uk), or visit the Museum of North Craven Life. South to Skipton offers the chance to visit Skipton Castle, one of England's most complete medieval castles (www.skiptoncastle.co.uk), and the children will love a steam ride on the Embsay and Bolton Abbey Steam Railway (www.embsayboltonabbeyrailway.org.uk).

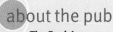

about the pub

The Buck Inn
Malham, Skipton
North Yorkshire BD23 4DA
Tel: 01729 830317
www.buckinnmalham.co.uk

DIRECTIONS: see Getting to the Start; pub is close to the river bridge in Malham village	
PARKING: 20	
OPEN: daily; all day May to October	
FOOD: daily	
BREWERY/COMPANY: free house	
REAL ALE: Theakston Best, Timothy Taylor Landlord, Copper Dragon beers	
DOGS: welcome in Hikers Bar and garden	
ROOMS: 10 en suite	

Along the canal at Gargrave

WALK

Gargrave

NORTH YORKSHIRE

Following the Leeds and Liverpool Canal from Gargrave.

Gargrave

Gargrave has long been a stopping-off point for travellers from the cities of West Yorkshire on their way to the coast at Morecambe or to the Lake District. These days, most visitors arrive along the A65 from Skipton, the route formerly taken by horse-drawn coaches. There is still evidence of the village's importance as a coaching centre, especially at the Old Swan Inn. Its position beside the River Aire had also proved important when 18th- and 19th-century surveyors were seeking westward routes for other methods of transport. The walk crosses the railway not long after leaving Gargrave; this is the route that, not far west, becomes the famous Settle-to-Carlisle line. And you will return to the village beside the Leeds and Liverpool Canal.

Although Gargrave is today mostly a 19th-century settlement, there is evidence that the area has been in occupation much longer. The site of a Roman villa has been identified near by, while excavation on West Street has found the remains of a moated homestead dating from the 13th century, with a smithy and a lime pit, that was reused in the 15th century. By the 18th century there were cotton mills in Gargrave, served by the canal, and weavers were engaged in producing cloth for the clothing industry. Their expertise resulted in the establishment here of one of the village's biggest employers, Johnson & Johnson Medical, where they found workers who could undertake the fine weaving that was needed to produce their bandages.

the walk

1 Turn left out of the car park and follow North Street back towards the village, passing the **Old Swan Inn** where you turn

The Leeds and Liverpool Canal at Gargrave

right along the main road. At the Aire Bridge turn left to pass the church. Just past **Church Close House** on your right, turn right, following the Pennine Way sign. Go over a stone stile in the wall on your left.

2 Follow the side of the wall, along the **Pennine Way** path, which is partly paved here. Go ahead across the field to a waymarked stile, then half left to another stile. Walk towards the top left-hand corner of the field to a stile that leads to **Mosber Lane** near a railway bridge.

3 Turn left, going over a bridge over the railway, then follow the track through a gateway and climb the hill. After the cattle grid, go over a stile on the left and follow the **Pennine Way** path across the field to meet another track. Where this track turns left, go straight ahead for 20yds (18.3m) to a signpost.

4 At the post, turn right, soon to walk below the wire fence, to reach a waymarked gate in a crossing fence. Go ahead across the field to a pair of gates. Take the waymarked left-hand one and continue ahead, at first with a fence on your right.

5 After meeting a **farm track** at the end of the next field follow it down to the canal by **Bank Newton Locks**. Cross the bridge and turn right along the tow path. The path passes through a gate and goes on to a road.

A cross on the village green at Gargrave

1h30 · **3.5 MILES** · **5.7 KM** · **LEVEL 1**23

MAP: OS Explorer OL2 Yorkshire Dales – Southern & Western

START/FINISH: Car park in North Street, Gargrave, opposite the village hall; grid ref: SD 932543

PATHS: field paths and tracks, then canal tow path, 4 stiles

LANDSCAPE: farmland and canal side

PUBLIC TOILETS: by bridge in Gargrave

TOURIST INFORMATION: Skipton, tel 01756 792809

THE PUB: Anchor Inn, Gargrave

🛈 The main road in Gargrave is usually very busy. The deep waters of the canal present a danger for small children

Getting to the start

Gargrave lies on the A65 Leeds to Kendal road 5 miles (8km) northwest of Skipton. Coming from the Skipton, turn right along North Street by the Old Swan Inn (left if you're coming from Kendal). The car park is on the right at the top of the road.

Researched and written by:
John Gillham, David Winpenny

Gargrave

NORTH YORKSHIRE

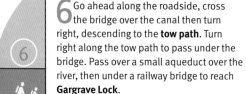

6 Go ahead along the roadside, cross the bridge over the canal then turn right, descending to the **tow path**. Turn right along the tow path to pass under the bridge. Pass over a small aqueduct over the river, then under a railway bridge to reach **Gargrave Lock**.

7 Beyond the lock, opposite the Anchor Inn, go under the road bridge and continue along the tow path to reach **Bridge 170**, at Higherland Lock. The Anchor Inn can be reached by going over a footbridge by the lock, otherwise go on to the road by a signpost.

8 Turn right down the road, and follow it back to the car park.

what to look for

It's worth looking closely at the locks as you walk along the canalside. Bank Newton Locks and the others along this stretch of the canal have the usual paddles, operated by a crank-operated gear, to open the ground holes at the base of the lock gates. At Higherland Lock, however, reached just before you leave the canal, there is a much simpler method. Beside the gates there are apparently two more, rather badly made, gates. These are the barriers that protect the ground holes, and they are simply pushed aside to let the water through. Look out along the way, too, for the iron markers that detail the distance between Liverpool and Leeds, and the elegant iron signposts. The bridge by which you regain the tow path after a short section along the road is designed to enable the towing horse to change from one side of the canal to the other.

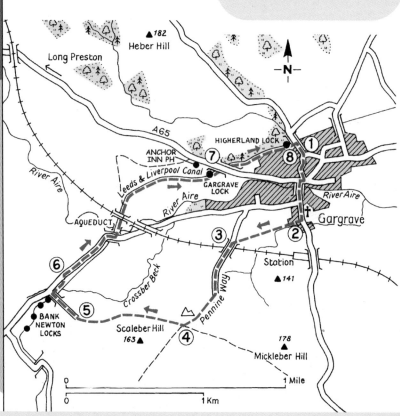

Anchor Inn

about the pub

Anchor Inn
Gargrave, Skipton
North Yorkshire BD23 3NA
Tel: 01756 749666

DIRECTIONS: beside the canal and the A65 north west of the town centre (Point 7)

PARKING: 200

OPEN: daily; all day

FOOD: daily; all day

BREWERY/COMPANY: Whitbread

REAL ALE: changing guest beers

DOGS: not allowed inside

This large stone and whitewash Brewers Fayre pub is beautifully sited by the canal locks, not far from Gargrave, and is extremely popular with families. It is decorated in typical corporate style with large compartmentalised rooms on differing levels. There is a children's play area and also seating outside the pub.

Food

A 'light bite' menu is served from noon until 6pm and includes sandwiches and home-made soups. Full meals focus on family favourites like fish and chips, gammon and egg, casseroles, pies, pasta dishes and roast lunches. Daily specials are chalked up on the blackboard.

Family facilities

Children can expect a warm welcome. The big garden has a good play area to keep youngsters amused on fine summer days. Inside, there are high chairs, baby-changing facilities and a children's menu.

Alternative refreshment stops

Gargrave has several restaurants, tea shops and cafés, including the Dalesman Café and the Bridge Restaurant. The Old Swan Inn on the A65 serves meals at lunchtimes and in the evenings.

☛ Where to go from here

Explore more canal history at nearby Skipton, where the Leeds and Liverpool runs through the heart of the old town. You should also visit the castle, one of the best preserved and most complete medieval castles in England (www.skiptoncastle.co.uk). Take a nostalgic trip on the Embsay and Bolton Abbey Steam Railway (www.embsaybolton abbeyrailway.org.uk), or visit magnificent Malham Cove.

From Arncliffe to Kettlewell

From unspoiled Arncliffe to Kettlewell, and back by the River Skirfare.

Littondale

The village of Arncliffe and the limestone scars surrounding it may look familiar to long-time followers of the television soap opera *Emmerdale*, for the opening titles for many years featured views of the village, and in the programme's very early days it was used as a film location. The cameras have long departed, leaving visitors space to appreciate Arncliffe's spectacular setting. Great limestone scars – once the home to eagles who gave the village its name – line the hillsides all around, and the fells are riddled with caves and gulleys. Arncliffe sits on a great spit of gravel, above the floodplain of the River Skirfare. Before the building of the bridge, a ford allowed travellers an easy crossing for the many ancient tracks that converge here. Evidence of Celtic field systems and stone enclosures south of the village suggests that some of these tracks may be prehistoric.

St Oswald's Church may have been Saxon in origin, but nothing remains of that or its Norman successor. The tower is 15th century, while the rest was rebuilt during the 18th and 19th centuries. The village records stretch back a long way, however; the church retains a list of 34 men from the

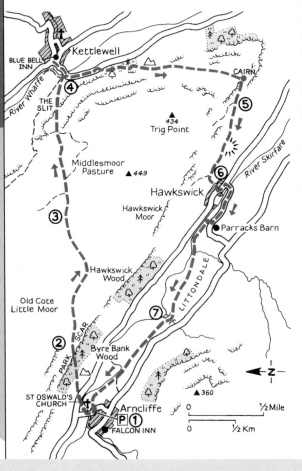

Arncliffe

NORTH YORKSHIRE

parish who went north from here in 1513 to fight the Scots at the Battle of Flodden – some of their names are still held by village families.

the walk

1 With your back to the **Falcon Inn**, turn right past the green, then left to pass the church. Cross the bridge and turn right at its end, over a gated stile. Walk parallel with the river and go up steps to cross the road via two stiles. Turn half right and follow a clear path steeply uphill across pastureland. The path maintains its direction as it climbs over smoothed limestone (slippery after rainfall) through the woods up **Park Scar** to a stile.

2 Beyond, follow the well-defined footpath, still maintaining its direction, across limestone-studded hillside to another ladder stile. Pass a signpost and go through a gap in a **tumbled wall** to another signpost. Continue to a ladder stile, then cross the corner of the field to another ladder stile at the ridge top.

3 The path descends to join a wall on the right. Ignore the prominent track going through a gate, but instead cross the wall lower down on a ladder stile. Follow the path beyond towards Kettlewell, descending steeply to a **signpost**. Cross a track to reach a limestone scar. Descend through a narrow cleft (**The Slit**), then walk down to a stile and, beyond it, a footpath sign. Turn right, go through a gate and on to the road. For refreshment, turn left over the bridge and into the village centre, where you'll see the **Blue Bell Inn** on the right-hand side of the road. Return to the same spot.

3h30 – **6.5 MILES** – **10.4 KM** – **LEVEL 1 2 3**

MAP: OS Explorer OL30 Yorkshire Dales – Northern & Central

START/FINISH: Arncliffe, near church; grid ref: SD 932719

PATHS: mostly clear, some rocky sections; may be muddy, 23 stiles

LANDSCAPE: rocky hillside, moorland and meadows

PUBLIC TOILETS: in Kettlewell (just off route)

TOURIST INFORMATION: Grassington, tel 01756 752774

THE PUB: Blue Bell Inn, Kettlewell

🛈 Steep and slippery limestone section above Arncliffe. Navigation could be difficult on the tops in hill fog – save for settled weather. A very short steep descent down the Slit (point 3)

Getting to the start

Arncliffe is Littondale's biggest village. It is usually reached by turning north from the A59 near Skipton along the B6160 'Grassington' road. Turn left just beyond the village of Kilnsey for 4 miles (6.4km). There's limited parking near the church and around the village green.

Researched and written by:
John Gillham, David Winpenny

Arncliffe

NORTH YORKSHIRE

4 Back at the far side of the main bridge, head south for 300yds (274m), then go right through a gate signed '**Hawkswick**'. Climb through woodland, go through a waymarked gate, then turn half right through a gap in the wall, passing a **ruined farm building** and its enclosure. Continue uphill, winding steeply to a gap in a wall beside a ladder stile. Bear left to another stile then ascend the grassy path beneath limestone crags and boulders to cross a stile in the ridge wall. With **Littondale** now in view, continue downhill, bending right by a cairn.

5 A sunken grassy track descends from the right to join the path. Follow it downhill with a wall on your left. Go through a gated stile and into **Hawkswick** village. Turn left at the junction to follow an unsurfaced lane, which then bends right between buildings before reaching the main valley road.

6 Cross and follow the road, bending right. Just before farm buildings on the left, turn right towards the footbridge; do not cross, but turn left at the **'Arncliffe'** sign to follow a well-defined riverside path. Eventually the path leaves the riverside and reaches a gate. It all but disappears

The village of Kettlewell nestled below the bulk of Great Whernside

in a large field, but the riverbank eventually meanders back to guide the route to another **footbridge**.

7 Walk to the right of a **barn** and go through a gate, then bear left to a squeeze stile in a crossing wall. Cross a track and go through three more stiles, following the river, to go through a gate near a house. Follow the waymarked posts to a kissing gate and past the **churchyard** to the starting point.

what to look for

Take some time to explore the ancient village of Kettlewell. Its name means the stream in a narrow valley – the village is built alongside the Dowber Gill Beck as it tumbles into the River Wharfe. Towering over Kettlewell are the long ridges of limestone and the huge bulk of Great Whernside. A weekly market used to be held at Kettlewell, which was on one of the main coaching routes from London to the North – beyond the village the route went over into Coverdale and into Richmond. Three inns served the travellers, and now provide for the many tourists who flock here.

The Blue Bell Inn

Two whitewashed inns, The Blue Bell and the Racehorses, face each other in the heart of Kettlewell. The Blue Bell is a 17th-century coaching inn, now well known for its excellent pub food. It's a cosy, welcoming pub, where you can dine in candlelight in the restaurant, or in the bar, which has beamed ceilings, flagstone floors, traditional pub furniture and a log fire, which roars in winter from a brick and stone fireplace. Benches and brollies on a rear terrace with lovely valley views for summer alfresco drinking.

about the pub

The Blue Bell Inn
Kettlewell, Skipton
North Yorkshire BD23 5QX
Tel: 01756 760230
www.bluebellinn.co.uk

DIRECTIONS:	beside the river bridge and B6160 in the village centre
PARKING:	7
OPEN:	daily; all year
FOOD:	daily
BREWERY/COMPANY:	free house
REAL ALE:	Theakston Best and Old Peculier, Tetley, Black Sheep Best
DOGS:	allowed in the pub
ROOMS:	7 en suite

Arncliffe

NORTH YORKSHIRE

Food
Extensive menus make good use of beef, lamb, trout and seasonal game from the Dales, seafood from the east coast, and fresh vegetables and herbs. Specialities include slow-roasted lamb shank and breast of chicken stuffed with Wensleydale cheese and wrapped in bacon.

Family facilities
Families are welcome at the pub. There's a family dining area, a standard children's menu, and a family bedroom sleeping four upstairs.

Alternative refreshment stops
For an authentic Dales experience, visit the Falcon Inn in Arncliffe, run by the same family for four generations. Here you'll be served good beer direct from the barrel. There are no pumps, pot jugs are filled at the barrel and the ale is poured from them into your glass.

☞ Where to go from here
Explore further up Littondale. The village of Litton is sited where the valley narrows, while beyond is the hamlet of Halton Gill. An 18th-century curate here, the Revd Miles Wilson, wrote a book to explain astronomy to ordinary folk. In *The Man in the Moon* he imagines a cobbler climbing to the moon from the top of Pen-y-ghent, then wandering at will around the solar system.

Calderdale and the Rochdale Canal

Take an easy tow-path ride through West Yorkshire's industrial heritage.

The Rochdale Canal

Like most northern valleys, Calderdale used to be a swamp, choked with scrub alder trees. For centuries packhorse trains carried by Galloway ponies had tramped the Pennine high roads, linking the mill villages like Mankinholes, Heptonstall, and Sowerby. The Industrial Revolution changed all that. Fast transportation became the watchword as new heavy industries flourished. The valleys were cleared and drained, with new roads and towns built. The idea for the Rochdale Canal was first mooted in 1766 when James Brindley was asked to undertake a survey. It wasn't until 1794, 22 years after Brindley's death, that the necessary Act of Parliament was passed. The 33 mile (53km) canal, designed by William Jessop, would extend the existing Calder and Hebble Navigation through Todmorden and Rochdale to link with the Bridgewater Canal at Castlefield in Manchester. Upland reservoirs had to be constructed to feed the 92 locks before the first trans-Pennine canal opened in 1804.

The railways came. In 1841 George Stephenson surveyed and built a line parallel to the canal. Initially, the combination worked well and the annual goods passing through by barge had reached 686,000 tons. By the 20th century, however, the tonnage had declined. In 1952 the canal closed. Happily, that was not the end of the story, for the 1980s and 90s saw the restoration of the canal – this time for leisure activities.

Calderdale

WEST YORKSHIRE

the ride

1 There's access to the canal at the back of the car park where you turn left along the tow path, past old mill buildings. On the initial stages the shapely hill of **Stoodley Pike** and its obelisk monument looms large on the horizon. You'll see many houseboats moored on Veever's Wharf just outside the town – many have their own canalside gardens. Take care when rounding the canal locks hereabouts for the gates protrude across the tow path. High on a hillside to the left the gaunt soot-stained church at **Cross Stone** offers a stark contrast to the stone-built canalside terraces with their pretty cottage gardens. The River Calder closes in on the canal, and before long you find yourself cycling on a narrow tree-lined island between the two watercourses.

2 Just beyond **Holmcoat Lock No 14** the tow path joins a tarred lane for a short stretch before descending back to the canalside. Take care here. At **Charlestown** pass the sewage works as quickly as possible! Just beyond the works the route is crossed by the Pennine Way long-distance path. For those in need of early refreshment, the tow path goes right by the **Stubbing Wharf pub**, which has tables outside in the summer, then the canal café. Next to the latter there's the Hebden Bridge Alternative Technology Centre.

3 On reaching Hebden Bridge proper you climb to and cross a **humpback bridge**, beyond which the tow path continues on the opposite bank, between the canal and a park (with toilets). However, you will probably wish to take a look around this

The Rochdale Canal flowing through the mill town of Hebden Bridge

4h00 | 18 MILES | 29 KM | LEVEL 1 2 3

MAP: OS Explorer OL21 South Pennines

START/FINISH: Lever Street car park, Todmorden; grid ref: SD 938241

TRAILS/TRACKS: narrow canal tow path

LANDSCAPE: mill towns, woodland and a semi-rural valley

PUBLIC TOILETS: the park at Hebden Bridge, and car park at Tuel Lock, Sowerby Bridge

TOURIST INFORMATION: Hebden Bridge, tel 01422 843831

CYCLE HIRE: none locally

THE PUB: Shoulder of Mutton, Mytholmroyd

❗ Unsuitable for small children. Take care under bridges: dismount if not confident. Permit needed to cycle tow paths (download from www.waterscape.com/cycling)

pleasant mill town. This is also a good turning point for cyclists with limited time or with young children. The wharf here has been restored and is usually highlighted by smart, brightly coloured longboats.

4 A mile (1.6km) beyond the town the tow path climbs out to the busy Halifax road to avoid a short tunnel. It's best to get off here and cross carefully. There's a short track leading back to the canalside, which leads into **Mytholmroyd**. To get to the pub , leave the tow path and turn right along the road to the A road. Turn right again here, then left down New Road, signed 'to Cragg'.

5 Return to the tow path and continue past the **cricket club**. Beyond this there's a short but steady climb to reach a road near the apex of a bend. Cross with care and descend back to the tow path. You're back into the country again until **Luddenden Foot** where you'll need to get off to go down some steps in the tow path.

6 The tow path goes through the short **Hollins Mill Tunnel** where it's single file only. Give way to riders and walkers already in the tunnel. Beyond this you arrive at Sowerby Bridge. The **Tuel Lock** here is the deepest inland water lock in the UK. **Wainhouse Tower** is on the distant hill. Turn round and retrace your route back to the start or go back by train.

Getting to the start

Todmorden is at the junction of the A646 Burnley to Halifax Road and the A6033 to Rochdale. The car park is just east of the town centre along the Halifax Road. With your back to the town centre, turn right (south) along Union Street South, which leads to Lever Street Car Park. The railway runs parallel, with stations at Todmorden, Hebden Bridge, Mytholmroyd and Sowerby Bridge, so it is possible to cycle one way and get the train back.

Why do this cycle ride?

Ride through the history of the Industrial Revolution and transportation, past and present.

Researched and written by: John Gillham

Illingworth

Halifax

Sowerby Bridge

Norland Moor

284 ▲

Moor End

Mount Tabor

Warley Town

tunnel

A646

River Ryb...

A58

Wainstalls

Luddenden Foot

Sowerby

Luddenden

410 ▲

Luddenden Dean

Rochdale Canal

River Calder

6

Mill Bank

Midgley

Midgley Moor

401 ▲

Blackwood Common

383 ▲ Crow Hill

Mytholmroyd

5 **Shoulder of Mutton PH**

Cragg Vale

B6138

Chiserley

N

Bell House Moor

4

A646

Pecket Well

A6033

3 **Hebden Bridge**

Erringden Moor

Ble

Mo

Withens Moor

Heptonstall

Stubbing Wharf PH

PENNINE WAY

0   1mile

0   1km

Slack

Charlestown

Edge End Moor

320 ▲

402 ▲ **Stoodley Pike Monument**

420 ▲

Colden

2

Mankinholes

Langfield Common

Colden Water

Blackshaw Head

Cross Stone

Heptonstall

431 ▲

Moor

437 ▲

Todmorden

P START

1

Rochdale

Canal

Hear Side Moor

A646

Burnley

A6033

Rochdale

Walsde

Shoulder of Mutton

A typical Pennines pub, next to a trout stream, well situated for local walks and the popular Calderdale Way. It was associated with the infamous Crag Coiners, 18th-century forgers who made their own golden guineas. There's a display of memorabilia (coins and tools) relating to the Coiners above the fireplace in the spacious bar, which also features a rustic board and black-and-red tiled floor. There's a cosy, cottage-style dining room with low beams and dark wood furnishings, and a secure back yard for bikes.

Food
A menu featuring home-cooked dishes from fresh ingredients includes good-value snacks like sandwiches (served with chips), filled jacket potatoes and burger and chips. Main meals include beef in ale pie, Cumberland sausages, steak and onion pie, a daily roast from the carvery, and up to ten vegetarian dishes.

Family facilities
Children are welcome inside and smaller portions of dishes are readily available. Sheltered garden beside the trout stream.

Alternative refreshment stops
The Stubbing Wharf pub beside the canal near Hebden Bridge and the Canal Café at Hebden Bridge.

Where to go from here
Drive up to see the attractive old weaving village of Heptonstall, above Hebden Bridge. Take the children to Eureka! The Museum for Children in Halifax, a fully interactive museum with over 400 'must touch' exhibits inviting you to take a journey of discovery through four main gallery spaces: Me and My Body, Living and Working Together, Our Global Garden and Invent, Create and Communicate (www.eureka.org.uk).

about the pub
Shoulder of Mutton
New Road, Mytholmroyd
Halifax, West Yorkshire HX7 5DZ
Tel: 01422 883165

DIRECTIONS: On B6138 in Mytholmroyd, opposite the railway station

PARKING: 16

OPEN: daily; all day Saturday and Sunday

FOOD: no food Tuesday evening

BREWERY/COMPANY: Enterprise Inns

REAL ALE: Caledonian Deuchars IPA, Timothy Taylor Landlord, Flowers IPA, Black Sheep Bitter, guest beers

Langthwaite in Arkengarthdale

Around an austere valley where hundreds of lead workers once toiled.

Arkengarthdale

The quiet villages of Arkle Town and Langthwaite are grey clusters of houses in the austere splendour of Arkengarthdale. One of the most northerly of the valleys in the Dales, it runs northwards from Swaledale into dark moorland, with the battle-scarred Stainmore beyond its head. This isolation and stillness is deceptive, however, for until the beginning of the 20th century the surrounding hills were mined for lead. The metal was first dug here in prehistoric times, but industrial mining of the great veins of lead really began in the 17th century. By 1628 there was a smelt mill beside the Slei Gill, which you will pass on the walk, and it is possible to pick out the evidence of some of the early miners' methods.

Booze (Norse for 'the house on the curved hillside') is now just a cluster of farm buildings, but was once a thriving mining community with more than 40 houses. Between Booze and Slei Gill you will pass the arched entrance to a level (a miners' tunnel) and behind it the remains of Tanner Rake Hush. This desolate valley is full of tumbled rock, left behind when the dammed stream at the top of the valley was allowed to rush down, exposing the lead

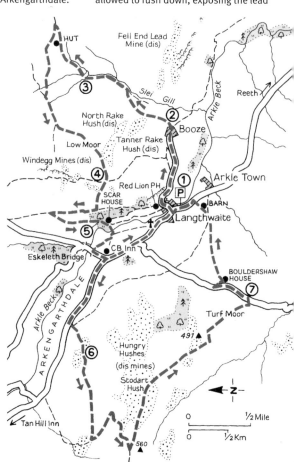

veins. You'll pass the spoil heaps of Windegg Mines, before returning to the valley near Scar House, now a shooting lodge owned by the Duke of Norfolk but once belonging to the mine master.

Near Eskeleth Bridge is the powder house, a small octagonal building, set safely by itself in a field. Built about 1804, it served the Octagon Smelt Mill, the remains of which can be traced near by. Just after you turn right along the road are the ruins of Langthwaite Smelt Mill.

the walk

1 Leave the car park, turn right, then right again into Langthwaite. Go over the bridge and continue ahead between cottages. Climb the hill and follow the lane to the hamlet of **Booze**. Pass the farmhouse and a **stone barn** and follow the track to a gate.

2 After the gate, where the track bends left, go straight on next to a broken wall. Bear right to go past a **ruined cottage**, then follow the path to the stream. Walk upstream, go through a gate and then cross the stream on stepping stones. Walk left on a faint path over the moorland.

3 Turn left along a gravel track beyond a **wooden hut**, then straight on along the grass track where the gravel track bends right. Turn left at a T-junction. Where the wall on your right ends, leave the track, bending right to a gate in the wall corner.

4 Follow the small gully downhill and go through a gate, where you turn right along a track and continue through a

| 3h15 | 8 MILES | 12.9 KM | LEVEL 1 2 3 |

SHORTER ALTERNATIVE ROUTE

| 2h00 | 4.5 MILES | 7.2 KM | LEVEL 1 2 3 |

MAP: OS Explorer OL30 Yorkshire Dales – Northern & Central

START/FINISH: pay-and-display car park at south end of Langthwaite village; grid ref: NZ 005024

PATHS: mostly clear tracks, some heather moor, 4 stiles

LANDSCAPE: mining-scarred moorland, with evocative remains of industry

PUBLIC TOILETS: none on route

TOURIST INFORMATION: Reeth, tel 01748 884059

THE PUB: The CB Inn, Arkengarthdale

❶ Full walk is long for young children – you can shorten the route at point 5. Navigation would be difficult in mist and low cloud

Getting to the start

To reach Langthwaite, follow the A6108 westwards from Richmond, then the B6270 as far as Reeth. At the top of the village green here, take the narrow lane signed 'Arkengarthdale'. The car park is on the south side of Langthwaite village.

Researched and written by:
John Gillham, David Winpenny

gateway and on to another track by a barn. Follow this track as it bends left by a stone wall and then passes farm buildings. Go through a small gate down a greasy track to a second gate, followed immediately by a gate into the **Scar House** grounds. Follow the drive as it bears right, downhill and over a bridge. Turn right along the track to a road.

5 The CB Inn is a diversion to the left down the road from here. If the weather has deteriorated or if you want to cut the route short, it's just a half mile down the road back to the start, otherwise turn left, back uphill, to a T-junction. Turn right and climb along the road. Where the road begins to level out (opposite an old **barn** on the right) turn left along a signed track.

6 At a gravelled area bear right (sketchy at first) to pick up a sunken green track that rakes uphill above **Moor Intake Farm**. The track meets a stony track high above a metal shed, and doubles back uphill with it before zigzagging to a group of **cairns** next to a large spoil heap. Turn left and follow the track across an area of spoil heaps. The track eventually follows the ridgetop, and is joined from the right by a shooters track that has come up from Bleaberry Gill (note the grouse butts). More **cairns** direct the track as it descends Turf Moor to the road.

7 Turn left along the road. Turn right at a bridleway sign by **Bouldershaw House**, then left just before the buildings. When halfway down the hill, go through a gate in the wall on the right and continue the descent. Beyond **Gill House** turn left across fields to reach the road. Turn left back to the car park.

The village of Langthwaite is the starting point of the walk

what to look for

Dry-stone walls are a typical feature of Arkengarthdale, as in much of the Yorkshire Dales. There are around 4,680 miles (7,530km) of such walls in the National Park, many of them built during the enclosure of former common land in the 17th to 19th centuries. These are the ones that head straight as an arrow for the fell tops. Earlier walls tend to enclose smaller fields and were built from rocks gathered from the fields – some may date from earlier than 1000 BC. They provide shelter for sheep and for smaller animals and birds, like whinchats. Many walls are derelict, and there are grants from various bodies available to farmers who want to repair them – a lack of skilled wallers is slowing down the work of repair.

The CB Inn

about the pub

The CB Inn
Arkengarthdale, Reeth
North Yorkshire DL11 6EN
Tel: 01748 884567
www.cbinn.co.uk

DIRECTIONS: see Getting to the Start; continue past Langthwaite to reach the pub on the right-hand side in a mile (1.6km)	
PARKING: 50	
OPEN: daily; all day; closed lunchtimes Monday to Thursday from December to February	
FOOD: daily	
BREWERY/COMPANY: free house	
REAL ALE: Theakston Bitter, John Smith's Cask, Black Sheep Bitter & Riggwelter	
DOGS: allowed in the bar	
ROOMS: 18 en suite	

Located in glorious Arkengarthdale, the most northerly of the Yorkshire Dales, this 18th-century inn is ideal for walkers, being close to the mid point of the Coast-to-Coast Walk. A popular hostelry, it is known throughout the area as the 'CB Inn', named after the son of Oliver Cromwell's physician (Charles Bathurst) who once owned lead mines in the area. The bar was originally a hay barn and stable for guests' horses, though it looks very different today with its antique pine furniture, stripped wood floors and roaring open fires. Accommodation is available in individually designed, en suite bedrooms with some stunning views.

Food

Excellent fresh fish, Swaledale lamb, and locally grown fruit and vegetables form the basis of the ever-changing menu. Typical of the dishes offered are five-fish fishcake, mussel chowder, shank of lamb on lentil potato cake with juniper jus, and (in season) roast grouse with ham and horseradish sauce. Filled baguettes and home-made soups are popular lunchtime snacks.

Family facilities

Children are welcome in the bars and overnight (extra beds). There's a children's menu and smaller portions of main meals are available, as are high chairs and drawing and colouring materials. If the weather's fine, head outside to the garden and play area.

Alternative refreshment stops

The Red Lion in Langthwaite has good beer and offers lunchtime bar food.

☞ Where to go from here

Continue up the road towards the head of Arkengarthdale and on to the 16th-century Tan Hill Inn, the highest pub in Britain at 1,732 feet (528m). In Swaledale, visit Hazel Brow Farm Visitor Centre at Low Row for guided tours, demonstrations, craft activities and much more (www.hazelbrow.co.uk), or learn more about the area through a visit to the Swaledale Folk Museum in Reeth.

CYCLE

Green ways of Wensleydale

Wensleydale NORTH YORKSHIRE

A glorious green terrace above one of the grandest of the Dales.

Bolton Castle

You hardly need to look for Bolton Castle. It dominates the landscape as you follow the road east of Carperby and towers over you as you toil up the lane of the main climb. The bulk of the castle dates back to 1399; it was established by Richard le Scrope, 1st Lord Scrope of Bolton and Lord Chancellor of England, and is still owned by his descendants. Much of the fabric is intact and there are rooms on five floors with furnishings and tableaux that give a vivid impression of what life in the castle was like. Mary Queen of Scots was imprisoned here for a time, though she was probably not too uncomfortable as she is said to have had 51 servants at her disposal! The castle grounds include a medieval garden, a herb garden and England's highest vineyard.

The old lead-mine site that is so conspicuous near the end of the off-road section is only one of many in the area, with the highest concentration being in nearby Swaledale. There is little to see in the way of buildings, shafts or levels here, just the large areas of bare spoil. The lack of vegetation colonising the ground indicates that there are significant residual concentrations of lead.

the ride

1 Cross the footbridge and follow a narrow tarmac path out to a wider, roughly surfaced lane. Bear right, cycle up to a road and turn right. About 2 miles (3.2km) beyond Carperby is a left turn signed for **Castle Bolton**, and the main climb of the route. Pass close under the corner of one of the **towers** and then at the top turn left, following signs for the car park and toilets.

2 Where the lane swings up into the car park, keep straight ahead through a gate and along an easy track. Follow the track through several gates and skirt to the left of some large **wooden farm sheds**; there can be muddy splashes here. After the next gate, the track becomes a little rougher, wiggling left through another gate and then right again. The track beyond is distinctly rougher, especially where it

14th-century Castle Bolton is visible on parts of the route

dips at a small **ford**; many people may
prefer to walk this short section.

3 At the next gate bear left above the
wall, on easy grassy going with some
wheel ruts and a few avoidable rocky
patches. After some perfect, almost lawn-
like grass, dip to a ford, sometimes dry but
still quite rough. More good grassy going
follows. At the next gate bear half left on a
smooth green track, following signs to
Askrigg and Carperby, which gives
delightful easy riding for the next 0.5 mile
(800m) to **Low Gate**.

4 At Low Gate go straight ahead up the
hill on more smooth green track, signed
for Askrigg. Level out and descend to a gate
where a rougher track (**Peatmoor Lane**)
crosses. Follow the green track ahead,
across a level grassy plateau, until it
descends to **Oxclose Gate**. From here the
track skirts to the left of the conspicuous
bare ground and spoil heaps on the site of
the **old lead mine**.

5 Opposite this the track acquires a good
gritty surface, and soon swings down to
a gate, with a **ford** just beyond. Wheel the
bikes across this and beware the drop just
below. Follow the stony track through
another gate. Beyond this a short section is
sometimes wet but can be avoided by
skirting to the right, crossing ruined walls.
Go up to another gate, swing left through it
and down 50yds (45.7m) to a signpost.

6 For the shorter loop, descend the
steep, twisting track to the little village
of **Woodhall**. The surface is loose in places,
and inexperienced riders should walk

— **2h00** — **12.5 MILES** — **20.1 KM** — **LEVEL 123** —

SHORTER ALTERNATIVE ROUTE

1h30 — **9.75 MILES** — **15.7 KM** — **LEVEL 123**

MAP: OS Explorer OL30 Yorkshire Dales –
Northern & Central

START/FINISH: small car park on A684 at
Aysgarth; grid ref: SD 995889

TRAILS/TRACKS: good grassy tracks; a few
short rough sections to be walked; return on
lanes which are muddy after rain

LANDSCAPE: high pasture and moorland
with views of broad pastoral dale

PUBLIC TOILETS: at Bolton Castle car park

TOURIST INFORMATION: Aysgarth Falls
National Park Centre, tel 01969 663424

CYCLE HIRE: none locally

THE PUB: The Wheatsheaf Hotel, Carperby

🛈 Basic loop: steep climb on road, short
sections of rough track, steep descent –
mountain bike recommended. Off-road
sections on longer loop are considerably
rougher and only for older, experienced
children – mountain bike essential.

Getting to the start

Aysgarth is on the main A684 road through
Wensleydale. Parking by arched footbridge
about 0.5 mile (800m) west of the village.

Why do this cycle ride?

Persevere as far as Low Gate and the real
worth of this ride becomes apparent. From
here on, you follow a magical green ribbon
of a bridleway along a broad terrace high
above the valley. Then you crest another
slight rise and more smooth grassy trails
unfurl ahead. When you get back to tarmac,
it's downhill nearly all the way.

Researched and written by: Jon Sparks

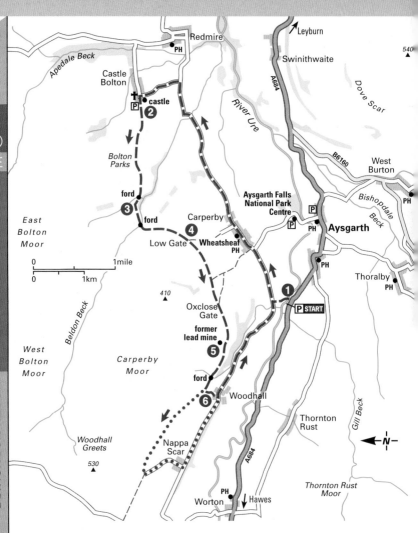

Redmire

PH

Leyburn

540

Swinithwaite

Apedale Beck

Castle
Bolton

castle

P

A684

Dove Scar

River Ure

Bolton
Parks

ford

Aysgarth Falls
National Park
Centre

P

West
Burton

B6160

ford

Carperby

Low Gate   Wheatsheaf
PH

P   PH   Aysgarth

Bishopdale Beck

PH

East
Bolton
Moor

0   1 mile

0   1 km

410

Oxclose
Gate

former
lead mine

START

P

PH

Thoralby

PH

West
Bolton
Moor

Beldon Beck

Carperby
Moor

ford

Woodhall

Thornton
Rust

Gill Beck

N

Woodhall
Greets

530

Nappa
Scar

A684

Thornton Rust
Moor

PH
Worton   Hawes

down. Turn left on the wider road for an easy run, almost entirely downhill, back to the start.

For the optional extension, turn right and climb the steep rough track. After two gates the gradient eases and the track winds through hummocks. Go through a gate alongside a **small plantation**. Beyond is the final climb, very tricky in places with bare rock and large loose stones; only experts will ride it all. Over the top there's

smooth friendly grass, then a final section of rutted track leads to a gate by a barn. The track beyond soon begins to descend, getting steeper and rougher. At a junction turn sharp left, almost immediately meeting tarmac. Follow the steep lane, which can have an overlay of loose grit in places, down into the hamlet of **Nappa Scar** and turn left on to the wider road.

The Wheatsheaf Hotel

The Wheatsheaf is quietly proud of a couple of its more famous guests. In 1941 it was the honeymoon location for Alf Wight – rather better known as 'James

Herriot' of All Creatures Great and Small fame. The following year it played host to an even more famous visitor in the shape of Greta Garbo, then performing a few miles away at Catterick Garrison. Garbo's legendary wish of 'I want to be alone' might be satisfied on the expansive moors above rather than in the sociable bar or the adjoining snug – which truly lives up to its name.

There is also a panelled dining room, and while you're there, do take a peek into the residents' lounge with its magnificent 17th-century fireplace. When the weather permits, there is outside seating at the front (south-facing) and there are more tables tucked in among shrubs and conifers behind the car park.

Food

Home-made dishes on the bar menu include giant Yorkshire puddings with various fillings, leek and parsnip hotpot, steak and bacon pie, Kilnsey trout with almonds, in addition to sandwiches and ploughman's lunches.

about the pub

The Wheatsheaf Hotel
Carperby, Leyburn
North Yorkshire DL8 4DF
Tel: 01969 663216
www.wheatsheafinwensleydale.co.uk

DIRECTIONS: village signposted off the A684 at Aysgarth
PARKING: 20
OPEN: daily; all day Saturday and Sunday; closed Monday lunchtime in winter
FOOD: daily
BREWERY/COMPANY: Black Sheep Brewery
REAL ALE: Black Sheep Best & Special, Websters Yorkshire Bitter
ROOMS: 8 en suite

Family facilities

Children are welcome in the pub and overnight (one family room), and there's a children's menu.

Alternative refreshment stops

The George & Dragon in Aysgarth village and a café at Aysgarth Falls National Park Visitor Centre.

☛ Where to go from here

Stop off at Bolton Castle (www.boltoncastle.co.uk); head for Hawes to visit the fascinating Dales Countryside Museum (www.destinationdales.org.uk); watch traditional ropemaking at the Hawes Ropemaker (www.ropemakers.co.uk); or learn about cheese-making at the Wensleydale Cheese Experience (www.wensleydale-creamery.co.uk).

WALK

West Burton

NORTH YORKSHIRE

From West Burton to Aysgarth

From West Burton to Aysgarth and back, via the famous Aysgarth Falls and some unusual farm buildings.

Aysgarth Village and Falls

Many regard West Burton as the prettiest village in the Dales. It is at the entrance to Bishopdale, with its road link to Wharfedale. South is the road to Walden Head, now a dead end for motorists, but for walkers an alternative route to Starbotton and Kettlewell. At the end of the walk you'll travel for a short time, near Flanders Hall, along Morpeth Gate, the old packhorse route to Middleham.

After crossing the wide flood plain of Bishopdale Beck, and crossing Eshington Bridge, you climb across the hill to descend into Aysgarth. A village of two halves, the larger part – which you come to first – is set along the A684 road. The walk takes you along the field path to Aysgarth's other half, around the church. Look inside at the spectacular choir screen from Jervaulx Abbey. Like the elaborate stall beside it, it was carved by the renowned Ripon workshops.

Beyond the church, the path follows the river beside Aysgarth's Middle and Lower Falls. They are now one of the most popular tourist sights in the Yorkshire Dales National Park.

On your return, you pass two oddities in the parkland behind the house at Sorrellsykes Park. These two follies were built in the 18th century by Mrs Sykes and no one seems to know why.

the walk

1 With your back to the Fox and Hounds turn left along the lane, past the Village Shop. Opposite 'Meadowcroft' go left through a ginnel, signed '**Eshington Bridge**'. Cross the road, turn right then left, through a gate and down steps. Pass the barn, go through a gateway and across the field. Go through a gap in the wall with a stile beyond, then bend right to a stile on to the road.

2 Turn left, go over the bridge and ahead up the narrow lane. As it bends left go ahead through a stile, signed '**Aysgarth**',

The Aysgarth Falls are a major attraction in the Yorkshire Dales National Park

then on through a gated stile. Go ahead to a gap in the fence near a **barn**, then through a gate. Bend left to a gate in the field corner, go through a gateway and on to a stile with a **footpath signpost**. Turn right and descend to another signpost, which points half right into a grassy hollow.

3 Go ahead to a stile in the field corner. Follow the signpost direction 'to Aysgarth' uphill to a gateway and go through a stile on the right. Cross the field half left to go through a gated stile on to a lane. Turn left, then almost immediately right through a stile, signed '**Aysgarth**'. Go through three stiles to a road.

4 Turn right into the village, past **The George & Dragon**. At the left bend, go ahead toward the Methodist church, then right at the green, and follow the lane. Go through a gate by **Field House** and to another stile, turning left along the track. Follow the path through eight stiles to the road.

5 Go ahead into the **churchyard**, pass right of the church and go through two stiles, through woodland, then over another stile. Follow the path downhill towards the river, descending steps to a gate, then a stile. When the footpath reaches the **river bank**, take a signed stile right.

6 Follow the path over two stiles to a signpost, bending right across the field to a road. Turn left over the bridge, turning right into **woodland** a few paces beyond,

MAP: OS Explorer OL30 Yorkshire Dales – Northern & Central

START/FINISH: centre of West Burton, by (but not on) the Green; grid ref: SE 017867

PATHS: field and riverside paths and tracks, 35 stiles

LANDSCAPE: two typical Dales villages, fields and falls on the River Ure

PUBLIC TOILETS: none on route; Aysgarth Falls National Park visitor centre is close

TOURIST INFORMATION: Leyburn, tel 01969 623069

THE PUB: The George & Dragon, Aysgarth

❶ The main road at Aysgarth can be very busy at the weekend

Getting to the start

West Burton lies at the convergence of Bishopdale and the Walden Valley. It's a mile south of the A684 Wensleydale road and can be accessed by taking the B6160 between West Witton and Aysgarth. There's no car park but there's plenty of space around the huge village green.

Researched and written by:
John Gillham, David Winpenny

A folly in the shape of a rocket ship on the grassy hills at Aysgarth

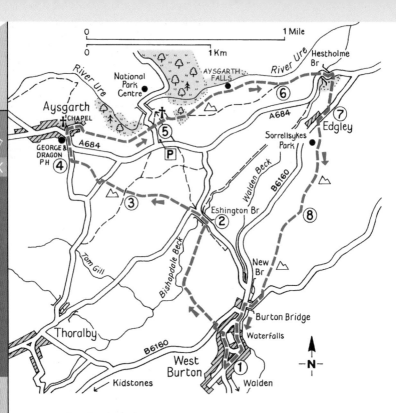

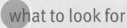

what to look for

The woods around Aysgarth have long been used for the production of hazel poles, and there is evidence of this trade on the walk, with the now-overgrown stumps of the hazel trees sprouting many branches, some of them of considerable age. In Freeholders' Wood beside the Middle and Lower Falls, on the opposite side of the River Ure from the route of the walk, the National Park Authority has restarted this ancient craft of coppicing. The name comes from the French couper, meaning to cut. Each year the hazel trees are cut back to a stump – called a stool – from which new shoots are allowed to grow. As long as they are protected from grazing cattle, the shoots develop into poles, and can be harvested after around seven years' growth. Hazel poles are traditionally used for making woven hurdles, and the thinner stems for basket-weaving.

signed '**Edgley**'. Go over a stile and cross the field to a gate on to the road.

7 Turn right. About 150yds (137m) along, go left over a stile, signed '**Flanders Hall**'. Walk below the follies to a footpath sign, beyond which the route crosses two tracks from the farming complex of **Sorrellsykes Park**. Past the last house, waymarking posts highlight the route which crosses a dyke, then passes above a copse of trees.

8 Opposite a **stone barn** on the hillside to the left, go right, through a gate, and go downhill through two more gates, then over three stiles to a lane. Turn right and go over a bridge to join the village road. Turn left, back to the Green.

The George & Dragon

Beautifully situated near the Aysgarth Falls in the heart of Herriot country, this attractive and very popular 17th-century coaching inn has a long tradition of offering warm Yorkshire hospitality. The small and cosy bar sports beams hung with tankards, jugs and copper pots, wood-panelled walls, built-in cushioned wall seats, and a warming winter log fire. Separate, plush lounge filled with antique china, and seven comfortable en suite bedrooms. Paved beer garden with lovely views of Upper Wensleydale.

Food

On the light lunch menu you will find sandwiches, ploughman's and popular snacks. More substantial dishes take in lamb chump with fondant potato, spring greens and lamb jus, loin of pork with caramelised apple and black pudding with mash, steamed monkfish, and battered haddock. Fresh fish dishes and Sunday roast lunches.

Family facilities

Smaller portions of the main menu dishes can be ordered and youngsters have a children's menu to choose from. There are two family bedrooms upstairs.

Alternative refreshment stops

Up the road from the church in Aysgarth, just off the route of the walk, the Palmer Flatt Hotel has bar meals and a restaurant, as well as a beer garden with views. In West Burton, the Fox and Hounds is a traditional village pub serving meals. Aysgarth Falls National Park Centre, across the river from the church, has a good coffee shop.

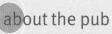

about the pub

The George & Dragon
Aysgarth, Leyburn
North Yorkshire DL8 3AD
Tel: 01969 663358
www.georgeanddragonaysgarth.co.uk

DIRECTIONS: beside the A68 in the centre of the village	
PARKING: 35	
OPEN: daily; all day	
FOOD: daily	
BREWERY/COMPANY: free house	
REAL ALE: Black Sheep Best & Special, John Smiths, Theakston Bitter	
DOGS: allowed in the bar	
ROOMS: 7 en suite	

☛ Where to go from here

Visit the Yorkshire Carriage Museum by the bridge below the church in Aysgarth. Housed in a former cotton mill that wove cloth for Garibaldi's 'Red Shirts', the revolutionary army of 19th-century Italy, the museum has a fascinating display of old-time transport, from carriages and carts to hearses and fire engines. The Dales Countryside Museum in Hawes (www.destinationdales.org) tells the story of the landscape and people of the Dales past and present, with hands-on exhibits for children.

West Burton   NORTH YORKSHIRE

Horsehouse and Coverdale

A moorside and riverside walk in one of the loveliest valleys in the Dales.

Horsehouse and Coverdale

It is hard to believe that the quiet village of Horsehouse was once bustling with traffic, as stagecoaches and packhorse trains passed through it on one of the main coaching routes from London to the North. Two inns served the travellers on their way to and from Richmond, a principal coaching centre. Beyond Horsehouse, to the south west, Coverdale grows steeper and wilder before the sharp drop down Park Rash into Kettlewell in Wharfedale – a descent that must have scared 17th- and 18th-century

Horsehouse   NORTH YORKSHIRE

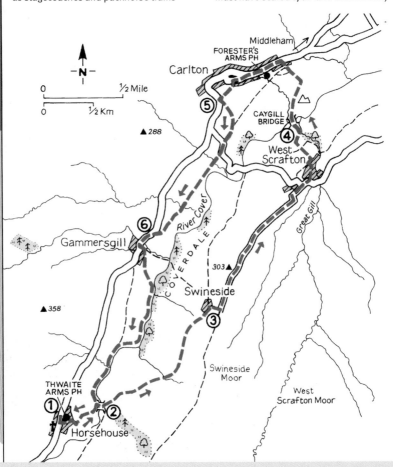

travellers. Pack-horses also used the route, bringing goods to the valley and taking lead and minerals from the mines on the moors.

Pedlars, too, followed the routes, and some met a gruesome end; three headless corpses were found by a side road into Nidderdale. Evidence suggested that they were Scottish pedlars, killed for their money and goods. Their heads were not found – nor were their murderers.

West Scrafton, a tiny village set beside Great Gill as it tumbles towards the River Cover below, is dominated by the heights of Great Roova Crags (1549ft/472m). Before the dissolution of the monasteries in the 1530s, the village was owned by the monks of Jervaulx Abbey. Much of the land was later owned by the Earl of Lennox; West Scrafton Manor House is said to have been the birthplace of his son Lord Darnley, murdered second husband of Mary, Queen of Scots and father of King James VI and I.

Carlton-in-Coverdale, the next village on the walk is the largest settlement in the

Harvesting the hay in Coverdale

2h30 — **6.5 MILES** — **10.4 KM** — **LEVEL 1 2 3**

WALK

MAP: OS Explorer OL30 Yorkshire Dales – Northern & Central

START/FINISH: roadside parking below former school in Horsehouse; grid ref: SE 047813

PATHS: field, moorland and riverside paths and tracks, 31 stiles

LANDSCAPE: farmed valley and moorland, with River Cover

PUBLIC TOILETS: none on route

TOURIST INFORMATION: Leyburn, tel 01969 623069

THE PUB: The Forester's Arms, Carlton

Getting to the start

Horsehouse in Coverdale lies on a remote and narrow road linking Kettlewell in Wharfedale with Middleham in Wensleydale. It's advisable and much easier to access the village from Wensleydale, where you should head south along a country lane just to the east of Wensley village.

Researched and written by:
John Gillham, David Winpenny

12

Horsehouse

NORTH YORKSHIRE

dale. Flatts Farm at the west end of the village has an inscription to Henry Constantine, 'The Coverdale Poet'.

Miles Coverdale, the first to translate the whole Bible into English, was born in the valley – no one knows exactly where – in 1488. The first edition of his Bible was published in Paris in 1535, and a revised version, known as the Great Bible, in 1538.

the walk

1 Walk past the **Thwaite Arms**, then curve behind it on a track. Turn right down a signed track, go through two gates, then bend left to a third gate. Beyond it bear half right to a gate and **footbridge**.

2 Cross the bridge and bear left. Go over a stile signed '**Swineside**', cross a small field to another stile then bear half right. Cross a track and follow a wall to a stile. Bear left, eventually on a path, through two stiles, then go half left to a signed stile. Climb the grassy path to a gap in the wall, then take the lower path, levelling out across **Rampshaw Bank**. Go through a stile and a gateway, then bend right to a gate, to the right of **Swineside Farm**.

3 After the gate, follow the track past the farmhouse then right, uphill. At the top, go over a cattle grid and follow the tarred

lane for 1.5 miles (2.4km) into **West Scrafton**. In the village take a track to the left signed 'No Through Road'. Turn left signed 'Carlton', then turn right. After a gate and a walled section, turn left down the field. Go through a kissing gate and right of a **barn**, towards Caygill Bridge. Bear right, following the wooded valley, through a gate and down to two **footbridges**.

4 After the bridges, go through a gate and ascend steeply, past a signpost. At the top bear right alongside a wall and on to a gate. Follow the footpath sign left, eventually reaching **Carlton**. Turn left along the road passing the **Forester's Arms**. Where it widens, bear left between cottages following a footpath sign to a stile. Continue through six more stiles to a road.

5 Turn left and go immediately through a gate. Descend to a stile, bear right above a **barn** to another stile and follow a wall to a stile on to a road. Turn left. At a left bend, go right, over a stile signed '**Gammersgill**'. Go over two more stiles and cross a stream (sometimes dry) and maintain direction across another field, passing to the left of a 5-bar gate then through a small waymarked gate. Cross the fields, going over a stile and a **wooden footbridge**, then follow an enclosed path. At the end of this turn half right across a field to a stile on to the road.

6 Turn left into **Gammersgill**, cross the bridge, then turn left through a gate signed '**Swineside**'. Bear right to another gate, then cross to a stile beside a gate. Bear half left to the field corner and go over a stile. Now follow the river over five more stiles and past a **stone bridge**. After another stile reach the footbridge crossed near the start of the walk. Retrace your steps back to **Horsehouse**.

what to look for

Like Middleham at the end of the valley, Coverdale is much given over to horses, with riding schools and livery stables throughout the dale. This is not a recent phenomenon – in Daniel Defoe's day the whole area was geared to the horse; in the third volume of his Tour through the Whole Island of Great Britain published in 1726, he wrote that 'all this country is full of jockeys, that is to say, dealers in horses, and breeders of horses…'

The Forester's Arms

about the pub

The Forester's Arms

Carlton, Leyburn
North Yorkshire DL8 4BB
Tel: 01969 640272

DIRECTIONS: see Getting to the Start; Carlton is 4.5 miles (7.2km) south west of Middleham and the A6108; pub is in the village centre

PARKING: 15

OPEN: all day Sunday; closed Mondays

FOOD: no food Sunday evening

BREWERY/COMPANY: free house

REAL ALE: Wensleydale Brewery beers

DOGS: allowed inside

ROOMS: 2 en suite

Stone-flagged floors, solid wooden furniture and a large, farmhouse-style fireplace add to the appeal of this fine old Dales pub hidden away in sleepy Coverdale. Built in 1630 of typical York stone, it has changed little over the years with its chunky oak beams and low ceilings, and careful refurbishment has successfully retained the historic and traditional atmosphere. Pretty, en suite bedrooms are available, with good views of the Dales, and there are lovely rural views from benches at the front of the inn.

Food

An imaginative menu lists such starters as Greek salad and garlic, chilli and parsley scallops and prawns, served with home-made bread, with main dishes ranging from roast belly pork with mash and cider gravy, rabbit stew and home-made fish cakes with dill *buerre blanc*, to battered haddock and chips, whole roast sea bass with dill hollandaise, and roast duck with marmalade sauce and sauté potatoes. Sandwiches available at lunchtime.

Family facilities

Children are welcome inside. Smaller portions of adult dishes are available.

Alternative refreshment stops

The Thwaite Arms in Horsehouse serves meals and has a reputation for its friendly atmosphere.

☞ Where to go from here

Visit the Forbidden Corner at Tupgill, 3 miles (4.8km) east of Carlton, a fantasy garden full of follies, tunnels, secret chambers and passages offering intrigue and unexpected discoveries for children. Open by timed ticket in advance only – call in at the tourist information centre in Leyburn. Take a look at Aysgarth Falls, the ruins of Jervaulx Abbey near East Witton, or enjoy a fascinating tour of the Black Sheep Brewery in Masham (www.blacksheep.co.uk).

River and woodland at Bolton Abbey

Over moorland and alongside the Strid to the romantic priory.

Bolton Abbey

Bolton Abbey has always been one of the showpieces of the Yorkshire Dales. The priory was built for Augustinian canons who founded their house here in 1154. This walk takes you a little further afield, and has the priory – it was never an abbey – as its climax. After passing under the archway you reach Bolton Hall, a hunting lodge for the Earls of Cumberland and their successors the Dukes of Devonshire. The walk then passes westwards through woodland to the top of a hill offering excellent views.

At the entrance to the woodland around the Strid, information boards explain the birds and plants here, including the sessile oak. Characteristic of the area, it is distinguished from the pedunculate oak by the fact that its acorns have no stalks. At the Strid itself the River Wharfe thunders through a narrow gorge between rocks.

The underlying geology is gritstone, with large white quartz pebbles embedded in it. The flow is fast and the river is 30ft (9m) deep here, so don't be tempted to cross; there have been many drownings.

A little further on is the Cavendish Pavilion. A survivor from the early 20th century, it has been restored and is still reminiscent of leisurely days in the 1920s.

the walk

1 Leave the car park at its north end, past the Village Store and the telephone box. Turn right, walk down the left side of the green, then turn left. Pass under an archway. Opposite the battlemented **Bolton Hall**, turn left on to a track through a signed gate. Where the track bends left, go through a

gate on the right with a bridleway sign. Cross the next field, aiming slightly left for a fingerpost to the right of some trees, then pass to the right of some **pools**. Continue through the gate beyond, and then turn right towards another gate into the wood.

2 Go through the gate and follow the clear track through the wood to the top gate out into a field. A **signpost** highlights the direction of the faint grass path across fields and towards some rounded **grassy hills**. In the second large field the path crosses a well-defined track to reach a gate in the wall corner. Beyond this turn right to follow a wall then climb a small hill, with wide views to the **Lower Barden Reservoir**

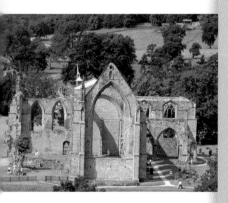

and the heather hills of **Barden Moor**. A prominent green path now descends gradually to the road.

3 Turn right along the road. After about 0.75 mile (1.2km) go right through a gate by a sign '**FP to B6160**'. Follow the path across sodden fields. The path meets and follows a wall on the left, then a

2h30 — **6.75 MILES** — **10.9 KM** — **LEVEL 1 2 3**

MAP: OS Explorer OL2 Yorkshire Dales – Southern & Western

START/FINISH: main pay car park at Bolton Abbey; grid ref: SE 071539

PATHS: field and moorland paths, then riverside paths, 4 stiles

LANDSCAPE: moorland with wide views and riverside woodland

PUBLIC TOILETS: by car park and at Cavendish Pavilion

TOURIST INFORMATION: Skipton, tel 01756 792809

THE PUB: Devonshire Arms Hotel (Brasserie), Bolton Abbey

🛈 Navigaton over moors would be difficult in poor weather. Dangerous river and currents around the Strid – read warning notices

Getting to the start

Bolton Abbey lies just to the north of the A59 between Skipton and Harrogate. Follow the B road past the Devonshire Arms. The main car park is on the left by the abbey and just before the village store.

Researched and written by:
John Gillham, David Winpenny

Top left: The white waters of the Strid, as the River Wharfe tumbles through rocks near Bolton Abbey
Left: The ruins of Bolton Abbey, which was founded in 1154

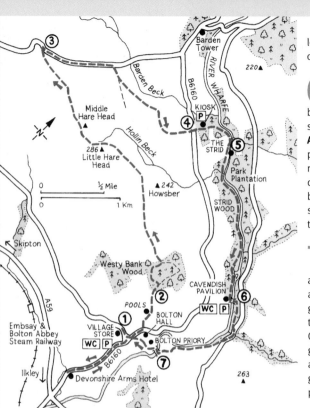

left by the café and go over the **footbridge**.

6 Immediately at the end of the bridge turn right signed '**Bolton Abbey'**. Follow the path parallel with the river, eventually descending to a bridge beside stepping-stones and the **priory**.

7 Cross the bridge and walk straight ahead up the slope and the steps to a gateway – known as the **Hole in the Wall**. Go through the gateway then straight ahead beside the green to reach the car park.

footpath diversion sign points the way left over a stone stile. Descend by a wall on the left to a roadside stile directly opposite to the **Strid car park**.

4 Cross the road, go through the car park and pass beside the **Strid Wood Nature Trails Kiosk**. Follow the most prominent path, signed 'The Strid'. Turn left just before **Lady Harriot's Seat** and descend to reach the riverbank where you turn right to reach the narrowest part of the river at the Strid.

5 From the Strid, continue on the riverside path until you reach an **information board** and gateway. Ignore the minor path signed Lud Stream and continue along the main track slanting away from the river to the **Cavendish Pavilion**. Go through a gate, turn

what to look for

Bolton Priory church is worth exploring. It is a mix of Norman and later styles – look out for the tell-tale round Norman arches and the pointed arches of the later work. The west front is very complicated – mainly because the tower was added just before the priory was shut. It has a huge, decorative window, but masks an even better 13th-century west front. The eastern end of the church – where the canons worshipped – is in ruins. The remains of the huge east window are one of the most memorable things about Bolton Priory. The nave, now the parish church, still gives an impression of the building's original grandeur. Notice the stained-glass windows on the right-hand side as you enter. They date from the first half of the 19th century and were designed, in convincing medieval style, by Augustus Pugin, whose decorative work is found in the Houses of Parliament.

Devonshire Arms Hotel (Brasserie)

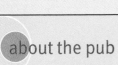

about the pub

Devonshire Arms Hotel (Brasserie)
Bolton Abbey, Skipton
North Yorkshire BD23 6AJ
Tel: 01756 710441
www.thedevonshirearms.co.uk

DIRECTIONS: see Getting to the Start	
PARKING: 150	
OPEN: daily; all day; closed afternoons Monday to Wednesday between October and March	
FOOD: daily; all day Sunday	
BREWERY/COMPANY: free house	
REAL ALE: Black Sheep Bitter, Wharfedale Folly Ale	
DOGS: allowed inside outside food times	
ROOMS: 41 en suite	

Set in the Wharfe valley close to Bolton Abbey, this former 17th-century coaching house is a stylish country house hotel with impressive bedrooms and a smart leisure club. Less formal, however, is the brasserie, with its polished wooden floorings, colourful modern art paintings on the walls, and a warm and friendly welcome to walkers and families. The bar is rather elegant, with comfortable easy chairs for those in need of a rest after their walk. There are many wooden tables on the patio to the rear of the Brasserie, for those who wish to dine outside or just relax with a cool drink. Besides the excellent (but quite expensive) main meals, sandwiches are available.

Food

Imaginative meals take in starter/main-course options like salmon fishcakes with lemon and lime mayonnaise and Moroccan chicken, lunchtime ploughman's and a smoked chicken, bacon and guacamole sandwich. Main dishes and specials may include saddle of rabbit with langoustines and capers and seared tuna on tomato, red onion and basil salad.

Family facilities

Families can expect a genuine welcome in the brasserie. There are high chairs and baby-changing facilities available, a small children's menu, and a cupboard full of games to keep children amused.

Alternative refreshment stops

Bolton Abbey is well supplied with places for a drink, a snack or a full meal. The Cavendish Pavilion has snacks, light meals and afternoon teas. The Priest's House at Barden Tower, about a mile (1.6km) north of the entrance to Strid Woods, has a restaurant and tea terrace.

☛ Where to go from here

Take a trip on the Embsay and Bolton Abbey Steam Railway, which has a station 1.5 miles (2.4km) south of the priory (www.embsayboltonabbeyrailway.org.uk). Explore Skipton and its medieval castle (www.skiptoncastle.co.uk), or view stalactites and stalagmites at Stump Cross Caverns at Greenhow near Pateley Bridge.

Along the wharfe from Addingham

From Addingham to Ilkley, along a stretch of the lovely River Wharfe.

Addingham and Ilkley

Addingham is not one of those compact Yorkshire villages that huddles around a village green. It used to be known as 'Long Addingham', and is actually made up of three separate communities that grew as the textile trades expanded. Within 50 years, from the end of the 17th century, Addingham's population went from 500 to 2,000. Though the mill was demolished in 1972, more houses were added to the mill-hands' cottages to create Low Mill Village, a pleasant riverside community.

Visitors from Bath or Cheltenham should feel quite at home in Ilkley, a town that seems to have more in common with Harrogate, its even posher neighbour to the north, than with the textile towns of West Yorkshire.

Like nearby Harrogate, Ilkley's fortunes changed dramatically with the discovery of medicinal springs. During the reign of Queen Victoria, the great and the good came here to 'take the waters' and socialise at the town's hydros and hotels. Visitor numbers increased with the coming of the railway, and included such luminaries as Madame Tussaud, George Bernard Shaw and Charles Darwin, taking a well-earned rest after the publication of *The Origin of Species*. With its open-air swimming pool and riverside promenades, Ilkley was an inland resort. Though we have replaced water cures with more sophisticated medicines, Ilkley remains a prosperous town, dedicated to the good things of life.

the walk

1 Walk 50yds (46m) up the road, and take stone steps down to the right, signed '**Dales Way**'. Bear immediately right again, and cross the River Wharfe on a **suspension bridge**. Follow a tarred path along a field edge. Cross a stream and join a metalled track between walls that soon emerges at a minor road by a sharp bend. Go right here; after about 0.5 mile (800m) of road walking you reach the little community of **Nesfield**.

2 About 200yds (183m) beyond the last house, and immediately after the road crosses a stream, bear left up a stony track (signed as a footpath to **High Austby**). Where the track turns left, immediately take a stile between two gates and cross the field ahead, keeping parallel to the road. Go through the top gate and follow the fence on the right to go through another gate next to an awkward stone stile. Follow the wall on your right. Beyond a small **conifer plantation**, take a ladder stile in the fence ahead to keep left of **Low Austby Farm**.

The old stone packhorse bridge at Ilkley

2h30	5.5 MILES	8.8 KM	LEVEL 1 2 3

MAP: OS Explorer 297 Lower Wharfedale

START/FINISH: lay-by at eastern end of Addingham, on bend where North Street becomes Bark Lane by information panel; grid ref: SE 084498

PATHS: riverside path and field paths, some road walking, 7 stiles

LANDSCAPE: rolling country and the River Wharfe

PUBLIC TOILETS: Ilkley

TOURIST INFORMATION: Ilkley, tel 01943 602319

THE PUB: The Fleece Inn, Addingham

❶ Short section by exposed riverbank just before Ilkley

Getting to the start

Addingham in Wharfedale lies halfway between Bolton Abbey and Ilkley. To get to the start of the walk from the north, turn left along the road by the village's first houses. The lay-by is on the left near the apex of a right-hand bend. From the south, leave the A65 road at the Addingham signpost, then take two right-hand forks to reach the same bend.

Researched and written by:
John Gillham, John Morrison

Addingham · WEST YORKSHIRE

3 Across the field cross a **footbridge** over a stream; beyond a stile you enter woodland. Follow a path downhill, leaving the wood by another step stile. Follow a fence uphill, then cross the middle of a field to locate a stile at the far end, to enter more **woodland**. Follow an obvious path through the trees, before reaching a road via a wall stile. Go right, downhill, to reach a road junction. Go right again, crossing Nesfield Road, and take a path to the left of an **electricity sub-station**. You have a few minutes of riverside walking before you reach **Ilkley's old stone bridge**.

4 Cross the bridge. This is your opportunity to explore the spa town of Ilkley. Otherwise you should turn right, immediately after the bridge, on to a **riverside path** (from here back to Addingham you are following the well-signed Dales Way). You soon continue along a lane, passing **Ilkley Lawn Tennis Club**. Opposite the clubhouse, take a footpath to the left, through a kissing gate, and across pasture.

The River Wharfe at Ilkley

You have seven more **kissing gates** to negotiate before you are back by the River Wharfe again. Cross a stream on a footbridge, and enter **woodland**. Cross another stream to meet a stony track. Go right, downhill, on this track to the river. Through another kissing gate, you follow a grassy path (with woodland and a fence to your left) before joining the **old A65 road**. Thanks to the bypass it is now almost empty of traffic.

5 Follow the road by the riverside. After almost 0.5 mile (800m) of road walking, go right, just before a row of **terraced houses**, on to **Old Lane**. Pass between the houses of a new development – **Low Mill Village** – to locate a riverside path, now metalled, at the far side. Once you have passed the **Rectory** on the left, and the grounds of the **Old Rectory** on your right, look for a kissing gate on the right. Take steps and follow the path to a tiny arched bridge over **Town Beck**. You have a grassy path across pasture, in front of the church. Join a tarred path that leads across another bridge, between houses, to re-emerge on **North Street** in Addingham. Turn right back to the lay-by or if you're going to the Fleece turn left, then right on to Main Street. The Fleece is in the village centre on the right-hand side of the road.

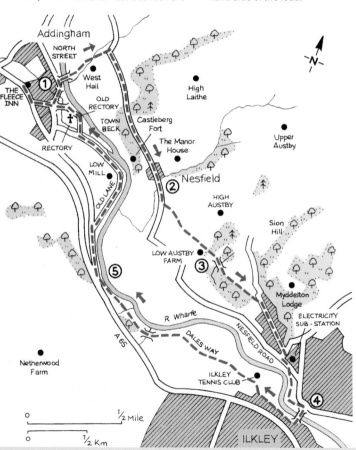

The Fleece Inn

Built around 1760 as a coaching house on the former site of the stocks, the Fleece Inn lies on the village's main street. In the early years the inn had an adjoining barn with accommodation for two cows. Today, it's more salubrious, with ivy and the colourful Virginia creeper covering the stone exterior walls. There are benches on the front pavement, some with large parasols, with well-kept hanging baskets enhancing the ambience. Inside you'll find a series of rooms on various levels, with stone-flagged floors, low ceilings, stone walls, an eclectic mix of old furnishings, and a big fireplace with a roaring log fire in winter. It serves some of the best pub food in Yorkshire, so come early if you're planning to eat.

about the pub

The Fleece Inn
154 Main Street, Addingham
Ilkley, West Yorkshire LS29 0LY
Tel: 01943 830491

DIRECTIONS: beside the A6160 in the village centre

PARKING: 20

OPEN: daily; all day

FOOD: daily; all day Sunday

BREWERY/COMPANY: Punch Taverns

REAL ALE: Timothy Taylor Landlord, Black Sheep Bitter, Tetley

DOGS: allowed in the bars and garden

Food
Excellent pub food ranges from light meals like sandwiches (beef with dripping or locally smoked salmon), and starters of grilled sardines, warm sausage and black pudding salad, or moules marinière. Hearty main dishes may feature Whitby fish pie, lamb hotpot, roast loin of pork, whole sea bass with vine tomatoes and basil, and Wharfedale rack of lamb with ratatouille. Round off with banana toffee pancakes or a plate of farmhouse cheeses.

Family facilities
Children are made welcome away from the bar. Above average children's menu (freshly prepared food) and a good-sized and safe garden for summer eating and drinking.

Alternative refreshment stops
In Addingham you could try the Sailor's Arms. At the bottom end of Ilkley you are close to the Riverside Hotel, which is particularly child-friendly.

☛ Where to go from here
Bolton Abbey, with its priory ruins in an idyllic setting by a bend in the River Wharfe (www.boltonabbey.com).

WALK

A circuit from Lofthouse

From Lofthouse to Ramsgill and Middlesmoor in the valley of the River Nidd.

Nidderdale

Nidderdale is a designated Area of Outstanding Natural Beauty. It is an area of moorland wildness and deep, farmed valleys. In the late 19th and 20th centuries parts of the dale were dammed as a chain of reservoirs was constructed to supply water to the city of Bradford.

Throughout Nidderdale are small, stone-built settlements like those visited on the walk – many of them of great antiquity. The monks of Fountains Abbey, near Ripon, founded the attractive village of Lofthouse as a grange in the Middle Ages. It was one of the bases from which they controlled their vast farming interests. Lofthouse now consists mainly of 19th-century cottages. Ramsgill, at the southern end of the route, is at the head of Gouthwaite Reservoir, which was opened in 1899 and is renowned for its spectacular bird life. The village was the birthplace, in

Left: Hilltop Middlesmoor village
Below right: A shady cobbled path in Middlesmoor village

1704, of Eugene Aram, scholar and murderer, who arranged for the slaughter of his wife's lover and was hanged for the crime.

In the third village, Middlesmoor, with its spectacular hilltop setting, the head of an Anglo-Saxon cross with its inscription to St Cedd in the church again indicates the age of the settlement.

It was once possible to travel from Pateley Bridge up the dale on the Nidd Valley Light Railway. It closed to passengers in 1929, but the track is still visible on much of the route.

the walk

1 Walk downhill past the Crown Hotel to the main road and turn left. Just beyond the drive for the **Old Vicarage**, go right, through a stile, signed the Nidderdale Way (the first of many waymarkers you'll see on this route). The path joins a short track to a gate, but instead of going through turn left, following a wall at first, then maintaining direction across a field. Over a stile at the far end turn half right to join the causeway of an **old railway**, which leads out to a roadside stile.

2 Cross the road and go through a gate. Follow the wire fence to a stile, then maintain direction across the field ahead. Before the next gateway, go left over a stile, avoiding the railway trackbed (private). Bear left and ascend, to a gate where a **Nidderdale Way** signpost highlights your direction towards the woods on the skyline. Through a kissing gate the path follows the lower edge of the woods. The narrow path passes above

Longsight House. Take the right fork track towards **Longsight Farm** to go left of the farmhouse. Follow the waymarkers to a wooden gate and ladder stile. Over the stile descend by a hedge on the left and go over a wooden bridge, where a gravel track leads past the buildings of **Bouthwaite** and out onto the road.

3 Turn right down the road to a T-junction. Turn left, over the bridge. Take the next track right, by the **triangular green**, then bear right again signed 'Stean'.

4 On reaching **West House Farm** go over a stile between the farm and a bungalow, cross the farm road and follow the waymarked posts, heading slightly left to join a track by **metal outbuildings**. The track heads up valley before raking down to a two-storey **barn**. From here a gravel track descends into a wooded valley and over a small bridge.

5 At a T-junction of tracks, turn left, uphill, and follow the walled track as it bends right. Beyond the approach road to **Moor House** the track becomes grassy. At a T-junction of tracks turn right. At the bottom, bend left above the **houses** and descend to the road at **Stean**.

MAP: OS Explorer OL30 Yorkshire Dales – Northern & Central

START/FINISH: car park by Memorial Hall in Lofthouse; grid ref: SE 101734

PATHS: mostly field paths and tracks; may be muddy, 20 stiles

LANDSCAPE: rich farmland and moorland, wide views from Middlesmoor

PUBLIC TOILETS: on main valley road at Lofthouse

TOURIST INFORMATION: Pateley Bridge, tel 01423 711147

THE PUB: Crown Hotel, Middlesmoor

A long walk for young children

Getting to the start

Lofthouse lies near the end of the Nidderdale road, 6 miles (9.7km) north west of Pateley Bridge. The best road heads north from the west side of Pateley Bridge. Turn right, uphill, in Lofthouse village to reach the car park, which is on the left. If that's full there is roadside parking on the moorland fringes above the village.

Researched and written by:
John Gillham, David Winpenny

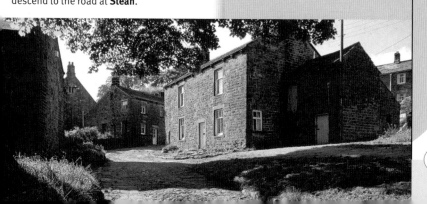

6 Beyond the **telephone box**, take a stile on the left signed 'Middlesmoor'. This descends to cross a bridge over **How Stean Gorge** then climbs the far banks to a gate. Beyond this go diagonally right across the field and over a stile. Now follow the wall uphill to the road. Turn left towards **Middlesmoor** where you'll find the Crown Hotel. Retrace your steps and turn left beside the **Wesleyan chapel** to the gateway of the parish church.

7 Turn right before the gate, through a stile signed 'Lofthouse'. Go down steps then through a stile and two gateways by **Halfway House**. Continue through a small gate then go diagonally left to a gate in the corner. In the lay-by go left on the nearside of the **cricket ground** to a laneside gate. Cross the lane and go over a bridge, then bear right to the centre of Lofthouse. Turn right to the car park.

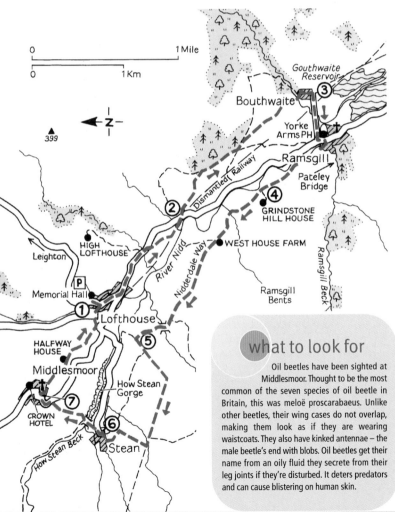

what to look for

Oil beetles have been sighted at Middlesmoor. Thought to be the most common of the seven species of oil beetle in Britain, this was meloë proscarabaeus. Unlike other beetles, their wing cases do not overlap, making them look as if they are wearing waistcoats. They also have kinked antennae – the male beetle's end with blobs. Oil beetles get their name from an oily fluid they secrete from their leg joints if they're disturbed. It deters predators and can cause blistering on human skin.

Crown Hotel

about the pub

Crown Hotel
Middlesmoor, Pateley Bridge
North Yorkshire HG3 5ST
Tel: 01423 755204

DIRECTIONS: see Getting to the Start and continue up valley to Middlesmoor for the Crown Hotel	
PARKING: 10	
OPEN: closed Monday lunchtime	
FOOD: daily	
BREWERY/COMPANY: free house	
REAL ALE: Black Sheep Bitter, Special & Emmerdale Ale, guest beer	
DOGS: allowed in the bar and garden	
ROOMS: 7 bedrooms (4 en suite)	

This remote and popular 17th-century stone-built pub at the top of the village has fine views over the rooftops towards the valley pastures and hills of Nidderdale and the distant Gouthwaite Reservoir. Ideal for those potholing or following the Nidderdale Way, it offers the chance to savour a refreshing pint of Black Sheep ale by roaring log fires in cosy and welcoming bars, or in the sunny garden in summer. Good value simple bedrooms.

Food

Good pub food ranges from decent sandwiches (home-cooked ham or beef) and cheese ploughman's to starters of black pudding, bacon and mash, home-made soups and garlic mushrooms. Main meals include lasagne, steak and ale pie, giant Yorkshire puddings filled with beef and vegetables, Nidderdale lamb chops, and salmon and broccoli pasta bake.

Family facilities

Children of all ages are welcome in the pub. There's a children's menu, smaller portions of adult dishes, and high chairs for younger family members.

Alternative refreshment stops

The Yorke Arms in Ramsgill serves top-of-the-range meals and enjoys an enviable reputation.

☞ Where to go from here

A visit to the attractive town of Pateley Bridge will prove rewarding. There are many fascinating small shops, as well as walks by the River Nidd and the interesting Nidderdale Museum in King Street, housed in a former workhouse, which illustrates the life and background of the Dales folk. Towards Ripon are the spectacular 12th-century remains of Fountains Abbey, the most complete Cistercian abbey in Britain (wwwfountainsabbey.org.uk).

Middleham Castle and the River Cover

From Middleham Castle, and back via the gallops for today's thoroughbreds.

Middleham

When Richard III died at the Battle of Bosworth Field in 1485, Middleham lost one of its favourite residents. Richard had lived here when a boy, and later set up home here. Middleham Castle today is a splendid ruin, with one of the biggest keeps in England, impressive curtain walls and a deep moat. From Middleham, the walk takes us to the River Cover and along its banks. After crossing Hullo Bridge the path ascends to Braithwaite Hall. Owned by the National Trust and open by appointment only, this is a modest farmhouse from 1667, with three fine gables and unusual oval windows beneath them. Inside are stone-flagged floors, a fine oak staircase and wood panelling all of the late 17th century.

After the Hall, the lane eventually crosses Coverham Bridge, probably built by the monks of nearby Coverham Abbey.

The few remains of the Abbey are mostly incorporated into later buildings.

For many people, Middleham is the home of famous racehorses, and you may be lucky enough to see some in training as you walk over Middleham Low Moor towards the end of the walk.

To your left as you leave the Low Moor and make your way back to the castle is William's Hill, the remains of the original motte and bailey castle built here by the Normans after 1066 to guard the approaches to Wensleydale and Coverdale.

the walk

1 From the cross in the Square, walk uphill past the Black Swan Hotel. A few paces beyond, turn left up a narrow passage beside the **Castle Tea Rooms**, continuing across the road and left of the **Castle** to a gate.

2 Climb half left across a huge field, following the sign pointing up the grassy hill. At the brow of the hill leave the path and

Middleham Castle in the Yorkshire Dales National Park dates back to the 12th century

aim half left again for the far left corner of the field. Cross the next three fields, over the waymarked stiles. After the third field, turn left to follow the **fence** running along the upper banks of the River Cover. Ignore a track doubling back right, but descend right at a waymark by a cross-wall, down to the bank of the river by the **stepping stones**.

3 Turn right (do not cross the stepping stones) and follow the **riverside path**, going through a gate and up some steps. After returning to the river bank, go right where the path forks to follow a **waymarked diversion**. Where the path appears to end by the river bank, turn right, uphill to a marker post.

4 Turn left and follow the upper edge of the **wood**, above the river. At the end of the field go left through a waymarked stile, through the trees to a second stile, then straight down the field back to the river bank. Go over a **waymarked stile** and onward to the bridge.

5 Go through the gate over the bridge. Follow the track as it winds right and uphill through two gates on to a road, opposite **Braithwaite Hall**. Turn right, and follow the road for a mile (1.6km) to **Coverham Bridge**. Turn right over the bridge, then right again.

6 Before the gates, turn left through a small gate, walk beside a waterfall and into the **churchyard**. Leave by the lychgate and turn left along the road. After 0.25 mile

MAP: OS Explorer OL30 Yorkshire Dales – Northern & Central
START/FINISH: In the Market Place, Middleham; grid ref: SE 127877
PATHS: field paths and tracks, with some road walking, 18 stiles
LANDSCAPE: gentle farmland, riverside paths, views of Wensleydale
PUBLIC TOILETS: Middleham
TOURIST INFORMATION: Leyburn, tel 01969 623069
THE PUB: Black Swan, Middleham
❶ A long walk for young children. Be alert for the training racehorses. The river bank poses a danger for small children

Getting to the start
Historic Middleham stands at the entrance to Wensleydale and Coverdale, just 3 miles (4.8km) south of Leyburn and 16 miles (25.8km) north west of Ripon on the A6108. There's parking by the market cross.

Researched and written by:
John Gillham, David Winpenny

River Cover flows gently through Coverdale

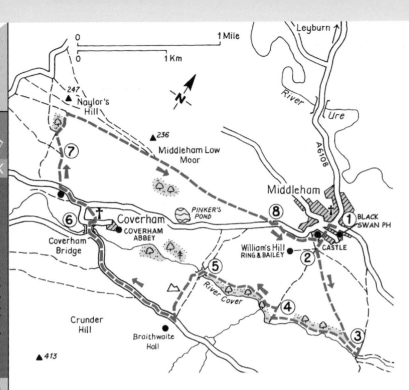

(400m) go through a gate on the right opposite a **disused factory**, bearing slightly left. Go over three stiles. Go through a gate, pass between buildings and go over three stiles through a belt of **woodland**.

7 Cross the field to a gateway right of the wood. After passing the **house**, bend left to a gate on to a track. Turn right, go through a gate and turn right again. Go right along the track at first, but where it veers slightly right, go straight ahead across the grassy moor. Aim for a **tree in a dip** and keep well to the right of the visible trig point. After passing to the right of (but not following) the **railings** and racehorse runs, the bridleway descends gently to the road.

8 Turn left. Just before the Middleham sign, take a signposted path on the right. Turn left over the stile and follow the path parallel to the road. Go through two

more stiles, then, by some **houses**, take another towards the castle, passing through a gate on to the lane. Turn left and return to the square.

what to look for

If you are very lucky you may see the iridescent blue and orange of the kingfisher, fishing above the waters of the River Cover. Vulnerable both to pollution and the ravages of a harsh winter, the kingfisher lives in the banks of the river, digging out a burrow up to 3ft (1m) deep. At the end a nest is constructed for the female to lay six or seven eggs. Young kingfishers are fed mainly with small fish – minnow and sticklebacks. Kingfishers catch fish with their fearsome bills and carry them back to their perches overlooking the stream. They carefully turn them so the head faces outwards from the bill, and hit them against the perch to stun or kill them, before swallowing them whole.

Black Swan

Dominated by the ruins of Middleham Castle, this welcoming Grade II listed inn dates back to 1670. Exposed beams, wooden panelling, high-backed settles and blazing winter log fires lend character to the stone-built property, which looks out across the market square in this famous horse-training area. Warm up following a winter walk with a pint of Old Peculier, a dark and strong ale tapped straight from wooden barrels. Accompany with good, hearty pub food. The rear garden backs onto the town's atmospheric castle ruins, which are floodlit on summer evenings.

Food

Traditional country cooking results in dishes like hearty casseroles (beef in Old Peculier), local steaks, rack of lamb with rosemary and redcurrant jus, roasted Kilnsey trout with parsley and thyme dressing, and game in season. Lighter bar meals range from soup and sandwiches to sausages and mash, chicken pie and classic lasagne.

Family facilities

Children are well catered for at the Black Swan. There's a standard 'junior selection' on the menu, high chairs, baby-changing facilities, and a family room with TV and children's videos. Upstairs, there is one family bedroom.

Alternative refreshment stops

Several of Middleham's hotels and inns offer meals and snacks as well as drinks. The White Swan has bar meals and a noted restaurant. Millers House Hotel has dinners (weekends only in winter). The Stable Door

about the pub

Black Swan
Market Place, Middleham
Leyburn, North Yorkshire DL8 4NP
Tel: 01969 622221

DIRECTIONS: see Getting to the start; pub on south side of Market Place beneath the castle	
PARKING: use Market Place	
OPEN: daily	
FOOD: daily	
BREWERY/COMPANY: free house	
REAL ALE: John Smith's, Theakston Best, Black Bull & Old Peculier, guest beer	
DOGS: allowed inside	
ROOMS: 7 en suite	

Restaurant is open most lunchtimes and evenings and offers good home-cooked food.

☛ Where to go from here

Head towards Ripon and take a fascinating tour of the Black Sheep Brewery in Masham (www.blacksheep.co.uk). Take a look at the ruins of Jervaulx Abbey, a Cistercian abbey established in 1156, on the way, or visit Fountains Abbey, the largest monastic ruin in Britain, and the landscaped gardens at Studley (www.nationaltrust.org.uk). Aysgarth Falls in Wensleydale are also worth seeing, especially after heavy rain.

From Esholt to the Five Rise Locks

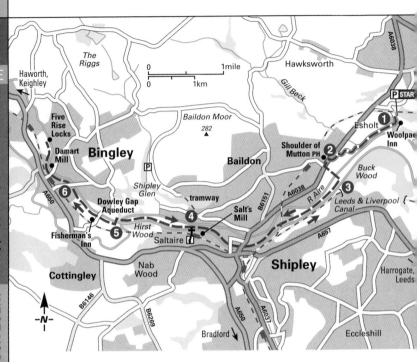

A slice of West Yorkshire from the rural environs of the TV series to the canalside mill towns of the Aire Valley.

Saltaire

Though the Industrial Revolution brought prosperity to the ruling classes, it also brought great inequalities. While the factory owners lived in their mansions in the country, their workers lived in overcrowded and unhygienic city streets. Wealthy Bradford mill owner Sir Titus Salt had been dismayed by this situation. He decided to move his mills into one unit, which would be built in a cleaner environment and would be part of a newly constructed model village. After finding his site at Shipley in the Aire Valley, Salt employed the best architects to design his project – Saltaire.

The village comprised 22 streets, all named after Salt's family members, and, on its completion in 1876, there were over 800 beautifully constructed houses in an area of 25 acres (10ha). Particularly notable are the beautiful Venetian-style Congregational church and the six-storey mill. The mill closed down in 1892, following a deep recession, and Saltaire lay idle and degenerating. However, almost a hundred years later a Leeds millionaire, Jonathan Silver, restored the mill, which now houses the 1853 Gallery with hundreds of exhibits

CYCLE

by local artist David Hockney. The village has been brought to life again with restaurants, a pub, antiques dealers and organised boat trips along the canal.

the ride

1 Turn left out of the car park on to the road (with care) and descend to the village. **The Woolpack**, post office and row of cottages, as featured for many years on the TV series *Emmerdale*, are on the left. Continue down the lane, passing the **Esholt Sports Club** and the campsite. The terraces of Bunker Hill on the right were *Emmerdale*'s Demdyke Row. Over a stone bridge and past a driving range the lane draws alongside the River Aire, then climbs right to meet the A6038 opposite the **Shoulder of Mutton pub**. It would be best to dismount here.

2 Turn left, following the footpath, then left again down **Buck Lane**. After a short way take the right fork, a mud and stone scrub-lined track that descends to the River Aire. Here a **steel bridge** built in 1889 takes you to the far bank, where the track climbs to reach the Leeds–Liverpool Canal at **Buck Wood**.

A visitors' farm at Esholt

MAP: OS Explorer 288 Bradford and Huddersfield

START/FINISH: Esholt; grid ref SE 182404

TRAILS/TRACKS: all quiet country lanes and tow path

LANDSCAPE: semi-rural and urban

PUBLIC TOILETS: Esholt car park and Five Rise Locks

TOURIST INFORMATION: Saltaire, tel 01274 774993

CYCLE HIRE: none locally

THE PUB: The Fisherman's Inn, Bingley

🛈 Busy road (A6038) at point 2; a steepish descent along the Buck Lane track to the river (point 2). Take care along the canal tow path

Getting to the start

Esholt lies on the north bank of the River Aire to the north east of Bradford. Follow the A650 trunk road to Shipley, then the A6038 through Baildon, before turning right for Esholt. The car park is on the hill, just to the north of the town and near the railway viaduct.

Why do this cycle ride?

This cycle ride visits some of the wonders of the Industrial Revolution, including Titus Salt's model village and the Bingley Five Rise Locks.

Researched and written by: John Gillham

Aire Valley   WEST YORKSHIRE

3 Turn right along the **tow path** here. After about 100yds (91m) you'll come across a **bench,** which some kind soul has sited right next to bushes that will in late August be endowed with some of the most luscious blackberries. We had a feast! The tow path is firm and wide at first, but beyond **bridge 209a,** carrying the railway to Baildon, it narrows considerably. If there are a lot of walkers about it would be best to follow the adjacent tarred lane and rejoin the tow path beyond the next bridge (209). Note: whichever way you choose, you'll be crossing traffic at this second bridge. At this point the canal is cutting through the industrial outskirts of Shipley, but soon things improve. Some smart **mill buildings** and a tower appear. You're entering the model mill town of Saltaire. Spend some time here; it's a fascinating place.

4 The tow path continues along a pleasing tree-lined section of the canal. Peeping through boughs on the left you'll see **Titus Salt's church.** At **Hirst Wood** beyond Saltaire, the River Aire and the canal draw close and the tow path continues on a narrow stretch of land between the two.

5 The canal finally crosses the river along the **Dowley Gap Aqueduct.** At bridge 206 the tow path on this side of the canal ends. Ride up the ramp, cross over the ridge, then descend to the tow path along the other side. At the next bridge **The Fisherman's Inn** has a beer garden.

6 The final stretch of the canal takes you through Bingley. There have been many changes here for the building of the Bingley Relief Road. After passing the huge **Damart Mill** and the three-rise staircase locks, you come to another tree-lined section before arriving at Bingley's famous **Five Rise Locks.** There's a steep but short climb to the top, but your reward is the fine view back to Bingley's woollen mills and chimneys and the chance of more refreshment at the lockside café. Retrace your route back along the canal to Esholt.

Five Rise Locks at Bingley

The Fisherman's Inn

Alternative refreshment stops
Before or after the ride you could try the Woolpack Inn at Esholt or, in Saltaire, there's Fanny's Café. In Bingley, there's the Five Rise Locks Café and Store.

☛ **Where to go from here**
You could take a walk along the signposted route from Saltaire to Shipley Glen, a popular picnic spot with a visitor centre and tramway up the hillside. For more information about the model mill town of Saltaire visit www.saltaire.yorks.com. Take a trip on the Keighley and Worth Valley Railway through the heart of Brontë country as it climbs to Haworth en route to Oxenhope. There are locomotive workshops at Haworth and an award-winning museum at Ingrow West (www.kwvr.co.uk).

An understated stone-built pub, conveniently sited right by the canal banks close to Bingley's famous Five Rise Locks. In summer there is a large attractive beer garden with wheelchair access and with pleasing views to the canal and across the Aire Valley. Very good standard of food, with a blackboard full of specials.

Food
Bar meals range from snacks and light bites to home-made pie of the day and sizzling steaks. Range of salads (chicken Caesar salad), ploughman's lunches, hot and cold sandwiches, filled jacket potatoes, gammon steak, and daily specials featuring fresh fish.

Family facilities
The pub has a children's certificate so they are very welcome throughout. There's a children's menu, smaller portions of main menu dishes and high chairs.

about the pub

The Fisherman's Inn
Wagon Lane, Dowley Gap, Bingley, West Yorkshire BD16 1TB
Tel 01274 561697

DIRECTIONS: follow the A650 through Shipley. Just beyond where this crosses the River Aire at Cottingley, turn right along Wagon Lane towards Dowley Gap. The pub is on the right beyond the bridge over the railway

PARKING: 20

OPEN: daily; all day

FOOD: no food Sunday evening

BREWERY/COMPANY: Enterprise Inns

REAL ALE: Tetley, guest beers

Richmond and Easby Abbey

Following in the steps of the Richmond Drummer, to Easby Abbey.

Richmond

The first part of the walk follows much of the route taken by the legendary Richmond Drummer Boy. At the end of the 18th century, the story says, soldiers discovered a tunnel that was thought to lead from there to Easby Abbey. They sent their drummer boy down it, beating his drum so they could follow from above ground. His route went under the Market Square and along to Frenchgate, then beside the river towards the abbey. At the spot now marked by the Drummer Boy Stone, the drumming stopped. The Drummer Boy was never seen again. The walk is re-enacted each year, with a local schoolboy playing the drum (but walking above ground!).

Easby Abbey, whose remains are seen on your walk, was founded in 1155. Just by the ruins is the parish church. It contains a replica of the Anglo-Saxon Easby Cross (the original is in the British Museum) and a set of medieval wall paintings.

After the abbey, you'll cross the River Swale on the old railway bridge, and follow the trackbed for a while. This was part of the branch line from Richmond to Darlington, which opened in 1846. It was closed in 1970. The station, a little further along the Catterick Road, is now a garden centre, and the engine shed a gym. Look right over Richmond Bridge as you cross, to see how the stonework differs from one end to the other. It was built by two different contractors. Between Points 5 and 6, you're following the old route of the Swale, which thousands of years ago changed its course and formed the hill known as Round Howe.

the walk

1 Leave the car park and turn right past the **cricket ground**, then left down Victoria Road to a roundabout where you go straight on down a narrow cobbled street. At the end turn left along Frenchgate, then fork right, down Station Road. Past **St Mary's Church**, go left along an unnamed street.

Richmond's castle standing on a rocky promontory above the River Swale

2h20 — **6 MILES** — **9.7 KM** — **LEVEL 2**

2 Turn right at the next junction and follow the track, passing immediately to the right of the **Drummer Boy Stone** along a waymarked path heading high above the River Swale towards **Easby Abbey**. As the abbey appears take a left fork across fields towards a wood. Turn right along the track and right again, this time down the metalled lane, which leads to the abbey entrance.

3 Go to the left of the **car park** along the track. Where it divides, keep on the higher path, then go right by **Platelayers Cottage** over the old railway bridge. Follow the track bed down to its terminus between Richmond's **swimming pool** and the bus depot.

4 Turn right along the main road for the short distance to **Station Bridge**. Go down the steps on the right, then follow the path that goes left under the bridge and climbs half left across fields to join Wainwright's **Coast to Coast route**, which comes in from the houses on the left. The path passes above woodland parallel to the river and follows the edge of some playing fields and a **clubhouse** before reaching a road.

5 Cross the road, and take a signed path opposite, to the left of the cottage. Climb steeply through the woodland of **Low Bank**, through a gate and a stile, bending right at the end of the woodland to a stile in a crossing fence. Turn right over the stile, and follow the signed path, above woodland at first, but then across the high pastures of **Round Howe**. A step-stile allows the path into the woods again. Turn left to

MAP: OS Explorer 304 Darlington & Richmond

START/FINISH: Nuns Close long-stay car park in Richmond; grid ref: NZ 168012

PATHS: field and riverside paths, a little town walking, 20 stiles

LANDSCAPE: valley of River Swale and its steep banks

PUBLIC TOILETS: Nuns Close car park and Round Howe car park

TOURIST INFORMATION: Richmond, tel 01748 850252

THE PUB: The Kings Head Hotel, Richmond

🛈 Take care on busy town streets

Getting to the start

Richmond is just 4 miles (6.4km) from Scotch Corner on the A1. Approaching from the A1, turn right at the roundabout by Friar Gardens, then right again by the Cricket Ground and Subaru garage. Nuns Close car park is on the left. From the west you'll see the long stay sign pointing left by the garage.

Researched and written by:
John Gillham, David Winpenny

follow a dilapidated wall at the top of the woods to a stile at a **crossroads of paths**.

6 Turn right, to go through a **5-bar gate**, then right again to follow the track as it bends downhill to cross a bridge over the Swale. Go left beyond the **car park** and left again at the main road. After 200yds (183m) go right up a **gravel track**, to a junction.

7 Turn right, and follow the track uphill, bearing right then left near the **farmhouse**, to reach a metalled lane. Turn right and follow the lane back into Richmond. Go ahead at the main road and follow it as it bends left to the **garage**, (turn left back to the car park). At the

what to look for

Wynds are a feature of the Richmond townscape. A northern term, from the Old English word for 'to spiral', these narrow lanes usually link two wider streets. Just after the parish church you will turn left along Lombard's Wynd. This was once part of the ancient route up from the river to Frenchgate – 'Frankesgate' in the Middle Ages. Both these names suggest that this part of the town was once occupied by foreign workers.

roundabout turn right down King Street, which will bring you into Market Square and by the side of the **Kings Head**.

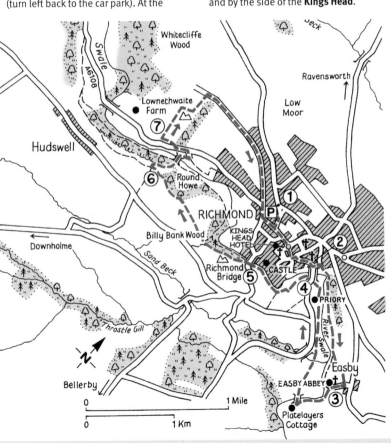

The Kings Head Hotel

In the heart of Richmond, overlooking the old cobbled town square, the historic Green Howards Regimental Museum and the Castle keep, is this old brick-built Georgian hotel, filled with big oil paintings, suits of armour, open log fires, and spacious bedrooms with all the amenities you require. Comfortable lounges are furnished with deep sofas and an interesting collection of antique clocks. Public rooms include a good local bar with plenty of buzz and atmosphere, hand-pulled ales and traditional bar meals. Afternoon tea is also worth sampling here.

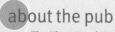

about the pub

The Kings Head Hotel
Market Place, Richmond
North Yorkshire DL10 4HS
Tel: 01748 850220
www.kingsheadrichmond.co.uk

DIRECTIONS: in the main square	
PARKING: in the main square in front of the hotel	
OPEN: daily; all day	
FOOD: daily	
BREWERY/COMPANY: free house	
REAL ALE: Black Sheep Bitter, Theakston Bitter, Boddingtons	
DOGS: welcome in reception but not in the bar	
ROOMS: 30 en suite	

Food

Good lunchtime meals range from hot and cold sandwiches, soups, ploughman's and taco bowls with salad (chicken and bacon), to deep-fried fresh haddock, pan-fried liver and bacon, and daily blackboard specials. Separate evening menu.

Family facilities

Children are welcome throughout the hotel. As well as high chairs, a family bedroom, and smaller portions of adult dishes, young children have their own menu to choose from.

Alternative refreshment stops

Richmond has many options for food and drink. One of the places that locals recommend is the Frenchgate Café, with its bistro-like atmosphere.

☛ Where to go from here

Visit Richmond Castle, which looms over the Swale Valley through much of the walk. Its keep, more than 100ft (30m) high, was complete by 1180. The castle now houses an exciting interactive exhibition (www.english-heritage.org.uk). The Green Howards Regimental Museum in Market Square can tell you more about the drummer boy and his regiment.

Upper Don Valley trail

CYCLE

Upper Don Valley

SOUTH YORKSHIRE

Exploring a valley emerging from an industrial past.

Trans-Pennine Trail

As numerous signs indicate, this route is part of the Trans-Pennine Trail (also encountered on rides 21 and 22). Described as the country's first multi-user long-distance route, it is open to walkers and cyclists throughout its length, with large sections also available to horse-riders and wheelchair users. The full distance, coast to coast, is 215 miles (346km), with extensions and branches adding up to a grand total of 350 miles (563km). The Trail is also part of the National Cycle Network and links to the E8 European long-distance path, which will eventually stretch all the way from the west coast of Ireland to Istanbul.

A stone's throw from the start is the eastern entrance to the Woodhead Tunnels. The first single-track tunnel was completed in 1845, with a second bore added in 1852. It is claimed that 3 per cent of the labourers working on the original tunnel lost their lives. Almost exactly 3 miles (4.8km) long, the original tunnels, from which smoke and fumes never cleared, were also unpopular with train crews on the open footplates of the steam engines. The line was part of the Great Central Railway, and later the London & North Eastern Railway before the railways were nationalised. A third, twin-track tunnel opened in 1953 and the line was electrified the following year. However, passenger traffic ceased in 1970 and the line finally closed in 1981.

Top: Upper Don Valley trail near Oxspring

the ride

1 From the bottom of the car park go through barriers and out on to the obvious trail. Bear right and drop down slightly on to the main line of the **old railway trackbed**. There is a sort of 'dual-carriageway' structure, with the intention being that the left-hand side is for cyclists and walkers, the right for horses. Even when there are no horses to be seen, 'their' side can be rougher (and pose certain other hazards!). Once past the **old station platforms**, the surroundings open out, with moorland up to the right. Go under the bridge on to a narrower section – single carriageway – and continue to **Hazlehead**. The old station buildings are now a private residence.

2 A bridge takes you over the A616. Pass a couple of smaller bridges and emerge on to a short elevated section. On the right, some obvious diggings are part of the old **Bullhouse colliery**. The most obvious feature is the **settlement lagoon**, part of a project to improve water quality of the river (a signboard explains all).

3 Pass some industrial buildings and a **wind turbine** on the colliery site, and cross a bridge above the A628. After a more open stretch, cross a lane. The barriers are tricky for adults to negotiate but small children can ride straight under them, so watch for traffic. Another track crosses the route and then an alternation of cuttings and open sections leads to a **recreation ground**, complete with skateboard park, on the outskirts of Penistone.

4 This section inevitably has a more urban feel but for the most part is surprisingly well insulated. Pass an **old engine shed** on the right, then go over a bridge, overlooked by the tower of the village church. Another cutting and another bridge lead to the overgrown platforms of **Penistone station**. Just beyond is the still-active railway line linking Huddersfield and Barnsley, with the current station away to the left. Follow the trail alongside the railway for about 0.5 mile (800m).

5 The railway swings away and the trail continues to pass under another bridge on the outskirts of **Oxspring**. At this point the trail divides. The left branch goes towards Barnsley, presently joining the Dove Valley Trail (see Route 22). If you don't want to go the full distance, you can follow this route down to the main road and a short way right to the Waggon and Horses at Oxspring.

6 Otherwise, keep straight ahead in the direction of Sheffield. Negotiate more barriers to cross a **farm track** and then cross a bridge high above the **River Don**. A sign warns of the tunnel ahead and then the cutting closes in. The trail may be muddy here, and the air can be considerably colder too. The **tunnel** itself is well lit but still has a certain dank and gloomy atmosphere. From its far end continue for about 600yds (549m), cross a bridge over a lane and reach some picnic tables. Drop down to the lane here and follow it left, under the trail, to reach the **Bridge Inn**. Once refreshed, you can retrace your tyre-tracks to the start. If you don't want to go back through the tunnel there is a waymarked alternative route.

3h00 | **20 MILES** | **32.2 KM** | **LEVEL 1**23

SHORTER ALTERNATIVE ROUTE

1h30 | **8.75 MILES** | **14.1 KM** | **LEVEL 1**23

MAP: OS Explorer OL1 Dark Peak

START/FINISH: car park at Dunford Bridge; grid ref: SE 158024

TRAILS/TRACKS: old railway track, mostly well-drained, occasionally muddy near far end point 1

LANDSCAPE: moorland, pastoral valley, woodland and some urban fringe

PUBLIC TOILETS: portaloo at start

TOURIST INFORMATION: Holmfirth, tel 01484 222444

CYCLE HIRE: The Bike Shed, Scissett, Huddersfield, tel 0800 018 4753

THE PUB: Bridge Inn, Thurgoland

🛈 Moderately steep ascent and descent on lane to pub at far point

Getting to the start

From Holmfirth, head south on B6106 for about 1.5 miles (2.4km) to Longley, fork right through Hade Edge and follow the road past several reservoirs into the Don valley. Large car park on the left just before the bridge.

Why do this cycle ride?

The Upper Don Valley Trail follows the former main line between Sheffield and Manchester. In its entirety, this is a long ride, and it's downhill all the way to Thurgoland – so it's uphill all the way back. The gradient is always gentle but it is persistent. Those looking for a shorter outing can turn round anywhere, but an obvious place to do so is on the outskirts of Penistone.

Researched and written by: Jon Sparks

Upper Don Valley

SOUTH YORKSHIRE

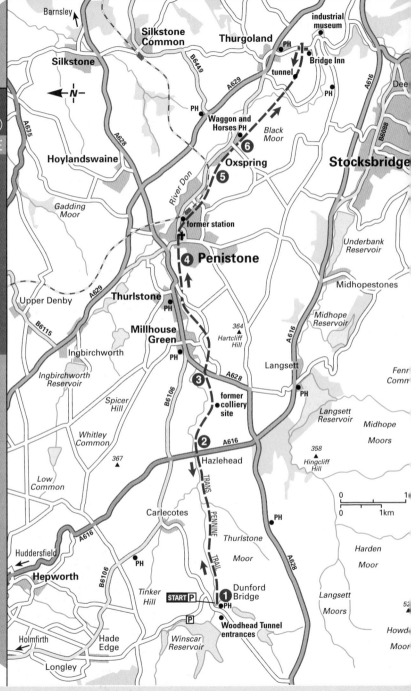

Upper Don Valley   SOUTH YORKSHIRE

Barnsley

Silkstone
Common

Thurgoland

industrial
museum

PH

Bridge Inn

Silkstone

tunnel

B6449

A629

PH

A616

Dee

Waggon and
Horses PH

6

Black
Moor

PH

B6088

Hoylandswaine

A635

A628

River Don

Oxspring

5

Stocksbridge

Gadding
Moor

former station

Underbank
Reservoir

Upper Denby

A629

4 Penistone

Midhopestones

B6115

Thurlstone

PH

364
▲
Hartcliff
Hill

Midhope
Reservoir

Millhouse
Green

PH

Langsett

Ingbirchworth

A628

Fenr
Comn

Ingbirchworth
Reservoir

B6106

3

former
colliery
site

Langsett
Reservoir

Midhope

Spicer
Hill

A616

PH

Moors

Whitley
Common

2

358
▲
Hingcliff
Hill

Midhope
Moors

Low
Common

367
▲

Hazlehead

Carlecotes

TRANS

PENNINE

Thurlstone
Moor

PH

Harden
Moor

Huddersfield

A616

PH

A628

Hepworth

B6106

Tinker
Hill

START P

1

Dunford
Bridge

PH

Langsett
Moors

52
▲

Holmfirth

Hade
Edge

P

Woodhead Tunnel
entrances

Winscar
Reservoir

Howde
Moor

Longley

0   1
0   1km

Bridge Inn

about the pub

Bridge Inn
Cote Lane, Thurgoland
Sheffield, South Yorkshire S35 7AE
Tel: 01142 2882016

DIRECTIONS:	beside the River Don, 0.5 mile (800m) south of the village centre and the A629
PARKING:	30
OPEN:	daily; all day
FOOD:	no food Sunday evening
BREWERY/COMPANY:	Enterprise Inns
REAL ALE:	Boddingtons, Tetley, guest beer

You have to leave the railway track to get to the Bridge Inn, but only for about 500yds (457m) of quiet lane – and there's the added novelty of being able to freewheel as you drop down slightly into the valley of the Don. In fact, if the weather is fine and you sit in the sheltered garden behind the pub, the loudest sound you'll hear is often the ripple of the river. Inside, a friendly welcome awaits. It's also useful to know that this solid stone-built pub is a very short distance from the Wortley Top Forge Industrial Museum.

Food
From a printed menu order crusty baguettes, starters like home-made soup, Greek salad and deep-fried mushrooms, and traditional main dishes such as large battered haddock and chips, gammon, egg and chips, steak and ale pie, venison sausages and mash, lasagne with garlic ciabatta, or rump steak with all the trimmings. Daily specials board.

Family facilities
Children are very welcome in the pub and a standard children's menu is available. Secluded and safe rear garden for summer eating and drinking.

Alternative refreshment stops
For those preferring to undertake the slightly shorter ride, the Waggon and Horses at Oxspring is a good refreshment stop. It is open all day and welcomes children (menu). There are also several pubs and cafés in Penistone.

☛ Where to go from here
Wortley Top Forge Industrial Museum (www.topforge.co.uk).

Harewood Estate   WEST YORKSHIRE

Harewood House and estate

A stately home with parkland by 'Capability' Brown, a few miles from Leeds.

Harewood Estate

The Harewood Estate passed through a number of hands during the 16th and 17th centuries, eventually being bought by the Lascelles family who still own the house. Edwin Lascelles left the 12th-century castle in its ruinous state but demolished the old hall. He wanted to create something special and hired the best architects and designers.

John Carr of York created a veritable palace of a house in an imposing neo-classical style, and laid out the estate village of Harewood too. The interior of the building was designed by Robert Adam. Thomas Chippendale made furniture for every room. The foundations were laid in 1759; 12 years later the house was finished. Inside are paintings by J M W Turner and Thomas Girtin. Turner was particularly taken with the area, producing pictures of many local landmarks. The sumptuous interior, full of portraits, ornate plasterwork and silk hangings, is in sharp contrast to life below stairs, in the kitchen and scullery.

The house sits in extensive grounds, which were groomed to be every bit as magnificent as the house. They were shaped by Lancelot 'Capability' Brown, the most renowned designer of the English landscape. In addition to the formal gardens, he created the lake and the woodland paths you will take on this walk.

Harewood House has had to earn its keep in recent years. The bird garden was the first commercial venture, but now the house hosts many events.

the walk

1 From the lay-by walk 50yds (46m) away from the village of Harewood, cross the busy road with care, and walk right, down the access track to **New Laithe Farm**. Keep to the left of the farm buildings, on a rutted track heading into the valley bottom. Go through two gates and bear half left up a field, towards **Hollin Hall**. Keep left of the buildings to pass **Hollin Hall Pond**.

2 Beyond the pond take a gate and follow a track to the left, uphill, skirting **woodland** before climbing half right by **gorse bushes** to a gate in the top corner of the field. Beyond this an enclosed track now continues the climb to the top of the hill.

3 Here it is joined by a grass track from the left and bends right (you are now joining the **Leeds Country Way**). Keep straight ahead when the track forks, through a gate. Skirt woodland to emerge at a road; bear right here to arrive at the main **A61**.

The south façade of Harewood House
overlooks a flower-covered parterre

3h00 — **6.5 MILES** — **10.5 KM** — **LEVEL 1** 23

MAP: OS Explorer 289 Leeds

START/FINISH: lay-by parking in Harewood; grid ref: SE 332450

PATHS: good paths and parkland tracks all the way, 2 stiles

LANDSCAPE: arable and parkland

PUBLIC TOILETS: none on route; in Harewood House if visiting

TOURIST INFORMATION: Wetherby, tel 01937 582151

THE PUB: The Harewood Arms, Harewood

🛑 Path passes deep water at Hollin Hill Pond. Very busy and fast roads to cross (A61 and A659)

Getting to the start

Harewood is 8 miles due north of Leeds on the junction of the A61 and the A659. The lay-by car parking lies on the north side of the A659, about a mile (1.6km) to the east of the village. When arriving from the east, the lay-by is the same distance past the fourth and last turn-off to East Hardwick.

Researched and written by:
John Gillham, John Morrison

WALK

Harewood Estate

WEST YORKSHIRE

4 Cross the road to enter the **Harewood Estate** (via the right-hand gate, between imposing gate-posts). Follow the broad track ahead, through landscaped parkland, soon getting views of Harewood House to the right. Enter **woodland** through a gate, bearing immediately left after a stone bridge.

5 Bear right after 100yds (91m), as the track forks. At a crossing of tracks, bear half right, downhill on a track signed **Ebor Way**. Turn right at the next junction, then take a left fork to pass in front of **Carr House**. Follow a good track down towards the lake. Go through a gate, keep left of a high **brick wall** and walk uphill to join a metalled access road to the left. Walk down past a **house** and keep straight ahead at crossroads. Cross a bridge and follow the lane up to a gate, soon passing **Home Farm** (now converted to business units).

6 Follow the road through pastureland, turning right at the T-junction. Continue through woodland and pasture until you come to the few **houses** that comprise the estate village of Harewood.

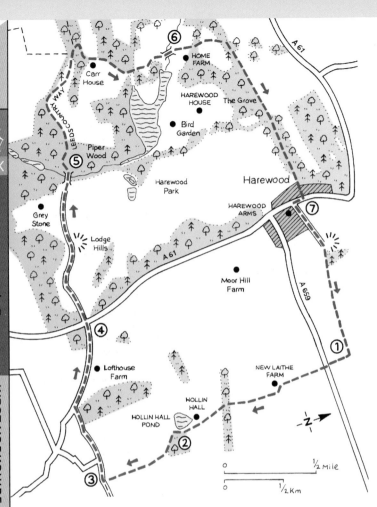

7 Cross the main A61 road with care and walk right, for just 50yds (46m), to take a metalled drive immediately before the Harewood Arms. Pass **Maltkiln House**, keeping straight on, through a gate, as the road becomes a track. Enjoy great views over Lower Wharfedale. Ignore the stile in the fence to your right and and stay with the pleasant track to a junction south of **Stockton Grange Farm**, where you turn right. This permissive bridleway takes you back to the A659 a few paces away from the lay-by.

what to look for

The red kite, a beautiful fork-tailed bird of prey, used to be a familiar sight. But the numbers had dwindled to just a few pairs, mostly in Wales, due to centuries of persecution. There is now a new initiative to reintroduce the red kite to Yorkshire, and a number of birds have been released at Harewood House. You may be lucky enough to spot one.

The Harewood Arms

Harewood Estate

WEST YORKSHIRE

about the pub

The Harewood Arms
Harrogate Road, Harewood
Leeds, West Yorkshire LS17 9LH
Tel: 0113 288 6566
www.harewoodarms.co.uk

DIRECTIONS: opposite the main gates to Harewood House in the village centre
PARKING: 100
OPEN: daily; all day
FOOD: daily; all day Saturday and Sunday
BREWERY/COMPANY: Samuel Smiths
REAL ALE: Samuel Smith's OBB
DOGS: allowed in the bar and garden
ROOMS: 23 en suite

Built in 1815, this former coaching inn stands opposite the gates to Harewood House and provides a smart and comfortable base for those visiting Harrogate, Leeds, York and the Dales.

Behind the rather foreboding stone façade of this Georgian hall lies a friendly pub serving excellent food. The carpeted lounge bar is extremely comfortable with many easy chairs, and Sam Smith's Old Brewery Bitter is hand-pulled from wooden casks. The restaurant serves à la carte and table d'hôte menus. Its Georgian windows look out on to the pleasant leafy back garden.

Food
In the bar tuck into various salads, sandwiches, filled baguettes, grilled Yorkshire gammon, omelettes, and local sausages and mash. In the restaurant, roast rack of lamb with redcurrant jus and sea bass with cream, white wine, prawn and fennel sauce show the style of cooking. Afternoon teas are also served.

Family facilties
Although there are no specific facilities for children, there is a family area in the bar and children are welcome overnight.

Alternative refreshment stops
If visiting Harewood House you will find a licensed café/restaurant.

☞ Where to go from here
While the walk described here uses rights of way through the grounds of Harewood House, you need to pay if you want to investigate the house itself, or the bird gardens, or the many other attractions that include an adventure playground. Make a day of it: do the walk in the morning, have lunch at the Harewood Arms and investigate the unrivalled splendour of Harewood House in the afternoon (www.harewood.org).

Wharncliffe Woods

CYCLE

Wharncliffe Woods

SOUTH YORKSHIRE

A taste of mountain biking in a hotbed of the sport.

Wharncliffe Woods

Mountain biking is a relatively young sport, its origins usually traced to California in the late 1970s, but has grown hugely in popularity and cross-country racing has been an Olympic discipline since 1996. But it's the downhill variety for which Wharncliffe Woods is most notable. Double World Cup downhill champion Steve Peat learned his trade in this area and has subsequently been among those responsible for the construction of some fearsome routes here. Serious downhillers require some highly specialised gear, including body protection and full-face helmets. The bikes, too, are specialised, with beefed-up suspension front and rear and powerful disc brakes. There is also a sub-sport known as freeride, which involves tackling the biggest possible jumps and drop-offs.

The Wharncliffe Woods area has been subject to quarrying for millennia, with evidence of Iron Age activity on Wharncliffe Crags; in fact the name Wharncliffe derives from the word 'quern', which is a small hand-operated grindstone mostly used in grinding grain for flour. The rock is, of course, millstone grit. The crags are now popular with rock-climbers. Later the woods were managed to provide fuel for the iron industry that flourished in the Don Valley from the 16th century onwards. Today Forest Enterprise continues to extract some timber commercially but the woods are increasingly managed for amenity and conservation and areas have been planted with broad-leaved native trees such as oak and birch.

the ride

1 From the car park turn left along the broad trail. At a collection of **signposts** turn right and then duck under a barrier on the left on to a narrower path. After another barrier the trail becomes broader again, descending gently through attractive **woods** of oak and birch. Negotiate another barrier and turn right on a track that descends more steeply. At the bottom of a particularly steep section is a **3-way bridleway sign**.

2 Turn right, and continue through more downhill sections. Cross a small wooden bridge, and duck under a barrier, back into **Wharncliffe Woods** proper.

3 Turn left and continue downhill, swinging right on to a more gently descending section of track. At a fork bear left, emerge on to a broad track, and immediately fork right, passing a Trans Pennine Trail sign for **Wortley**. Continue downhill, taking great care on a section with a very loose surface where another track joins from the left. As a second track comes in from the left, look up to the right and you can see the first of the **MTB downhill routes** emerging on to the main track.

4 Now there's a slight climb followed by some gentle undulations, bringing you into a densely wooded section and coming close to a **railway line** on the left. After more level riding there's a fork, with a **Trans Pennine Trail sign**. Follow this down the broader left branch, swinging back right and rising where a narrower track forks off to the left. Now begin a long gentle ascent,

Below: Wharncliffe Woods

which dips under power lines. Look out for **Wharncliffe Crags** on the right through the trees before a slight dip. The track levels out for a short way. When it begins to climb again look for a sharp right turn just beyond another Trans Pennine Trail sign. There are also signs for **Wharncliffe Heath nature reserve**.

5 The climb isn't excessively steep anywhere, but some sections are made really tricky by the surface, which is either loose sand, loose stones or a mixture. Anyone who completes the ascent without dismounting can claim to have passed the entry exam to real mountain biking. Keep straight on through a gap in a wall and along a more level sandy track, now with open **moorland** on the right and some fine mature **oak woods** on the left. After another short ascent, meet a slightly wider track and continue straight ahead. Just beyond this the path levels out, with the most expansive views of the entire ride. As you come back into woods, the track dips down, with quite a tricky section over rocks and mud, to a road.

1h30 — **7 MILES** — **11.3 KM** — **LEVEL 1 2 3**

CYCLE

MAP: OS Explorer 278 Sheffield & Barnsley
START/FINISH: Wharncliffe Woods car park; grid ref: SK 325951
TRAILS/TRACKS: mostly good forest tracks with a few narrower and/or rougher sections
LANDSCAPE: mature woodland, mostly coniferous plantations, with occasional views of farmland, heathland and crags
PUBLIC TOILETS: none on route
TOURIST INFORMATION: Sheffield, tel 01142 211900
CYCLE HIRE: Cycosport, Barnsley, tel 01226 204020
THE PUB: The Wortley Arms Hotel, Wortley
🛈 Some steep climbs and descents; beware some loose surfaces. For older, experienced children; mountain bike essential

Getting to the start
From M1 junction 36, follow the A61 towards Sheffield for 1.5 miles (2.4km), over a roundabout. Take the next right turn to Howbrook. Go left at the crossroads in the village. Follow this lane for about 0.5 mile (800m), crossing the A629, to reach a T-junction. Go left and in about 2 miles (3.2km) reach the main parking area for Wharncliffe Woods (on the right).

Why do this cycle ride?
Wharncliffe Woods is a name that dedicated mountain bikers recognise. Competitions are regularly held here. Our route doesn't involve anything extreme, but it does give a little of the flavour, with some fairly steep but well-surfaced descents, and a challenging climb. For a more straightforward ride, follow the green waymarked route from the car park.

Researched and written by: Jon Sparks

Wharncliffe Woods

SOUTH YORKSHIRE

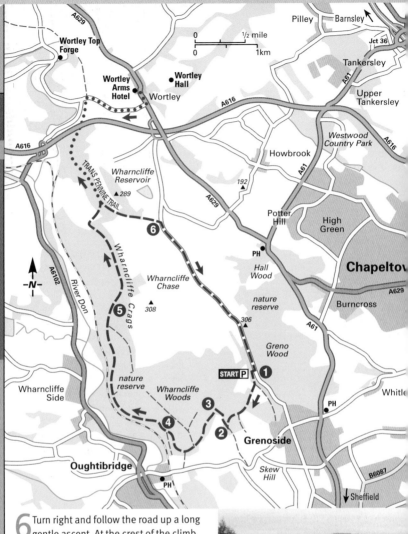

6 Turn right and follow the road up a long gentle ascent. At the crest of the climb, coming back to **woods** on the right, another **Trans Pennine Trail sign** indicates a track that leads back to the car park.

There's no pub right on the ride route, though it could fairly easily be extended by continuing along the Trans Pennine Trail for about another mile (1.6km); pass under the A616 then soon after drop down to a minor road and follow it east to the A629. Turn left into Wortley.

The Wortley Arms Hotel

The landlord of this rambling old village pub is well used to cyclists and walkers. The pub is an official Trans Pennine Trail Stamping Point (anyone riding or walking the full coast-to-coast route can obtain a card and get it stamped at various points along the route). Also, since it was formerly known as The Wharncliffe Arms, there couldn't be a much more appropriate choice for this ride. It's a solid stone building that was built on the site of an earlier hostelry in 1754, with the arms of the Earls of Wharncliffe carved in stone over the door. Many of the old materials were used in the construction and inside you can see some fine wood panelling, exposed stonework, wooden floors and low beams, while in the lounge bar there's a huge inglenook fireplace with a log fire in winter.

Food

The lounge bar menu lists good traditional pub food. Choices include an extensive list of sandwiches and baguettes, various salads and filled jacket potatoes, and main dishes such as cod and chips, steak and ale pie and a roast of the day.

Family facilities

Children are welcome in the bars. There are no play facilities but young children do have their own menu.

Alternative refreshment stops

None on the route. Plenty of hotels, cafés, pubs and restaurants in Sheffield.

☛ Where to go from here

Sheffield has much to offer the family. Visit Kelham Island Museum for the story of Sheffield, its industry and life (www.simt.co.uk), the Fire and Police Museum or the Sheffield Bus Museum. Nearer Wharncliffe and Wortley is Wortley Top Forge (www.topforge.co.uk), the last example of a working water-powered drop forge. You can also look round Wortley Hall Gardens.

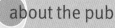

about the pub

The Wortley Arms Hotel
Halifax Road, Wortley
Sheffield, South Yorkshire S35 7DB
Tel: 01142 882245

DIRECTIONS: turn left from Wharncliffe Woods car park. At the junction of the A616 and A629, follow the A629 north for 0.5 mile (800m) to Wortley. Pub in village centre

PARKING: 30

OPEN: daily; all day

FOOD: daily; all day Saturday, Sunday until 6.30pm

BREWERY/COMPANY: free house

REAL ALE: Wortley Golden Best, Oakwell Barnsley Bitter, Black Sheep Bitter, Timothy Taylor Landlord, guest beers

ROOMS: 3 en suite

The Dove Valley trail

Dove Valley

SOUTH YORKSHIRE

Rural surprises in the heart of industrial South Yorkshire.

Wentworth Castle

Wentworth Castle is conspicuous soon after Point 3. Those doing the return through the lanes will pass much closer to it, but see little of the castle itself. They will, however, see some of the associated estate buildings. The present castle is largely the result of a massive programme of works in the early 18th century, instigated by Sir Thomas Wentworth, Earl of Strafford. He originally expected to inherit the estate at Wentworth Woodhouse, a few miles away, but it went to a cousin instead. Much of the motivation for all the grand works around Wentworth Castle seems to have been a burning desire to outshine his cousin's property. The castle is now home to the Northern College for Residential Adult Education. It is a Grade I listed building, but is probably less important than the surrounding gardens and parkland. These contain a fine iron conservatory and mock Gothic castle, which gained greater public prominence during the first (2003) series of the BBC2 programme *Restoration*, ultimately achieving third place in the final. The gardens are open to the public at limited times, mostly on weekend afternoons.

the ride

1 From the corner of the car park furthest from the road, a path leads via a ramp to a lane. Follow this right and down, then bear right before the **museum** and down past the **Field Study Centre**. Go over a couple of small bridges then turn left, with a sign to the Trans Pennine Trail. Follow the narrow track, rising quite steeply, keep straight ahead on tarmac, and finally go up alongside a gate to the **railway track** and turn left.

2 There's a short tree-lined section then it opens out, with views over the reservoir on the left. On the other side a short track and the crossing of a lane give access to **Wigfield Open Farm** and its café. Follow the rail track to a barrier. Go straight across the lane to the continuation of the track, alongside a small **car park**.

3 The surroundings are now pleasantly rural, but your ears tell you that the M1 is not far off. High on the left beyond the motorway is the impressive façade of **Wentworth Castle**. After a slightly narrower section, negotiate more barriers at the crossing of a narrow tarmac lane – or you can take the mountain bikers' route over humps. Soon after this you come out on to the **iron bridge** over the M1. High parapets, embellished with fine graffiti art, conceal the motorway from view. And very quickly, depending on wind direction, the noise fades.

4 Continue along the narrow trail through **young woods**, the trees meeting overhead in places. After crossing a sandy track, with more barriers, there's an open area, with masses of ragwort, **picnic tables**, and regular glimpses of open fields.

A sculpture on the Dove Valley trail

| 2h00 | 9 MILES | 14.5 KM | LEVEL 123 |

SHORTER ALTERNATIVE ROUTE

| 1h30 | 8.25 MILES | 13.3 KM | LEVEL 123 |

MAP: OS Explorer 278 Sheffield & Barnsley

START/FINISH: Worsbrough Country Park car park; grid ref: SE 352033

TRAILS/TRACKS: old railway tracks and short surfaced tracks through country park; alternative return on lanes

LANDSCAPE: reservoir and valley with mix of farmland and woodland

PUBLIC TOILETS: at Worsbrough Mill

TOURIST INFORMATION: Barnsley, tel 01226 206757

CYCLE HIRE: Cycosport, Barnsley, tel 01226 204020

THE PUB: Button Mill Inn, Barnsley

🛑 Some steep climbs and descents on return through lanes

Getting to the start

Leave the M1 at junction 36 and follow the A61 towards Barnsley. The Worsbrough Country Park car park is on the left as the road descends into the valley of the River Dove.

Why do this cycle ride?

This ride starts on the edge of Barnsley, and crosses the M1, so you might not expect to find peace and quiet, but the surroundings are almost entirely rural. It makes for a gentle ride, ideal for younger children, especially with the country park and open farm near the start. The more ambitious can take on the return through the lanes, which doesn't add much to the distance but does include a steep climb and descent.

Researched and written by: Jon Sparks

Dove Valley

SOUTH YORKSHIRE

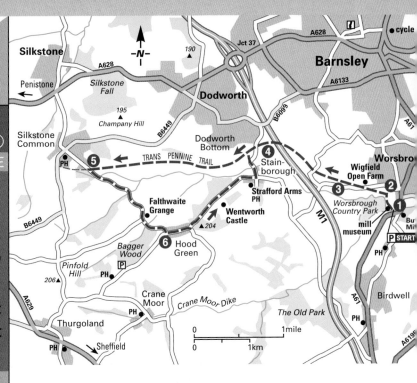

The track now begins to climb discernibly, and an elevated section takes you through more mature woods. Just before a bridge, with a road below, watch for a sign showing a cyclist, a pedestrian and a **British Rail symbol**. (It's possible to continue a little further but soon the line is blocked, before it enters the Silkstone tunnel. The Trans Pennine Trail continues from this point by the 'up and over path'.)

5 Either turn back along the rail track or follow the sign down a ramp to a lane and turn left. Descend past **Nabs Wood** (Woodland Trust) on the right, make a short climb, and swing left at the top of the rise, enjoying the more open views. Drop down again, go over the bridge and then climb once more. It soon eases off. Pass some fine, recently restored timber-framed buildings at **Falthwaite Grange**, keep left at a small junction, and then a slight dip leads all too

quickly into a very steep but not too long climb past **Bagger Wood** and into the village of **Hood Green**. At a T-junction where the road levels off, turn left.

6 At the far end of the village there's another short steep rise. Keep left at a junction. Continue through **woodland** with steep slopes dropping to the left, then descend quite steeply, into the village of **Stainborough**. As the road begins to level out there's a crossroads. (The alternative pub, the **Strafford Arms**, is a short way up to the right here.) Turn left and descend some more. Swing left by the entrance to **Strafford Industrial Park** then immediately fork right on to a rough track. This gets very rough on the final rise before rejoining the **old railway** at a Trans Pennine Trail sign. Turn right here to head back to the start.

Button Mill Inn

about the pub

Button Mill Inn
Park Road, Worsbrough Bridge
Barnsley, South Yorkshire S70 5LJ
Tel: 01226 282639

DIRECTIONS: see Getting to the Start; pub opposite the Country Park car park

PARKING: 40

OPEN: daily; all day

FOOD: daily; all day

BREWERY/COMPANY: FGL Pubs

REAL ALE: John Smiths's Bitter & Magnet

ROOMS: 6 en suite

Button Mill Inn couldn't be much more handily placed, just across the road from the car park (but cross with care, as it's a busy highway). It's a handsome, four-square sort of building, originally a coaching inn, dating from the 1840s, though today's interior has a more standardised pub feel to it. There's plenty of space, but it's broken into more manageable areas, helped by some small changes of level, and there is lots of comfortable seating, so overcrowding should rarely be a problem. A wide-ranging menu is served all day. One drawback is that outside seating is a bit limited: the tables at the front are very close to the busy road, while there are a few more at the back adjoining the car park.

Food
Food is traditional pub fare ranging from filled jacket potatoes and hot and cold sandwiches, to daily specials like duck in plum sauce, braised lamb shoulder and spicy beef fillet cooked Szechuan style.

Family facilities
Children are welcome in the bars and you'll find a children's menu for younger family members.

Alternative refreshment stops
Café at Wigfield Open Farm and the Strafford Arms in Stainborough (just off the longer loop).

☞ Where to go from here
In addition to exploring Worsbrough Country Park and Mill Museum and the Wigfield Open Farm, take a look at the magnificent gardens at Wentworth Castle (www.wentworthcastle.org).

The Harland Way

Follow a picturesque railway line to discover Yorkshire's forgotten fortress.

Around Spofforth

Lying among the peaceful pastures of the Crimple Valley, Spofforth is an idyllic backwater for a Sunday afternoon ride. Go back in time to the medieval era and things were very different. A year after the Battle of Hastings, William the Conqueror's friend, William de Percy, made Spofforth his headquarters. The original dwelling would have been a fortified hall, of which nothing remains, but by the 13th century the castle was taking shape, built into the rock on which it stood. Subsequent alterations of the 14th and 15th centuries gave the castle its powerful walls and that strong Gothic look.

In 1309 Henry de Percy bought the Manor of Alnwick in Northumberland and made that his main residence, but the family's alliances were to land them in trouble on several occasions – after their rebellion against King Henry IV in 1408, and their support in the Wars of the Roses. On both occasions the Crown confiscated Spofforth Castle. The castle lay waste for around a hundred years until Henry, Lord Percy restored it in 1559. Within another hundred years, however, it was sacked by Oliver Cromwell's forces during fierce fighting of the Civil War. Stand on the green

today, and you can still feel the presence and imagine the times of turmoil endured by this rugged historic building.

the ride

1 With your back to the car park entrance, turn right along the railway trackbed, highlighted by a **Harland Way fingerpost**. The line has been exploded through the bedrock to reveal limestone crags, now hung with pleasant woodland that offers excellent shade on hot summer days.

2 Take the left fork at the junction that used to be known as the **Wetherby Triangle**. You're soon joined from the right by another branch of the line and together the routes head west towards Spofforth. Halfway along the track you have to dismount to get through a **metal gateway**, then again almost immediately at another gate. The trackbed forges through an avenue of beech, hawthorn, ash, and rowan before coming out into the open. Now you'll see thickets of wild roses and bramble, with scabious and purple vetch among the numerous wild flowers of the verges. There are wide views across cornfields, and soon the tower of **Spofforth church** comes into view ahead.

3 The Harland Way ends beyond a gate just short of the village. A gravel path veers right across a green on to **East Park Road**. This threads through **modern housing** to come to the main road where you should turn right. If you have young

The grounds of ruined Spofforth Castle

2h00 · **8 MILES** · **12.9 KM** · **LEVEL 1 2 3**

MAP: OS Explorer 289 Leeds

START/FINISH: Sicklinghall Road, Wetherby; grid ref: SE 397483

TRAILS/TRACKS: well compacted gravel railway trackbed, lanes and smooth bridleways

LANDSCAPE: pastureland and village

PUBLIC TOILETS: none on route

TOURIST INFORMATION: Wetherby, tel 01937 582151

CYCLE HIRE: none locally

THE PUB: The Castle, Spofforth

⚠ A short section of main road through Spofforth village

Getting to the start

From the A661 Wetherby to Harrogate road turn off on the westbound Sicklinghall Road then after 300yds (274m) a blue cycleway sign points to the car park on the right.

Why do this cycle ride?

The Harland Way forms the basis of a delightful rural ride following in the tracks of the steam trains and visiting one of Yorkshire's most fascinating Norman castles.

Researched and written by: John Gillham

CYCLE

Harland Way

NORTH YORKSHIRE

children it might be better to dismount to cross the road, and use the pavements to get to **The Castle** inn.

4 Just beyond the pub, where the road bends right, take the lane on the left, which heads for the **castle**. When you've seen the castle retrace your route past the pub then turn right along Park Road. Beyond the **houses** this becomes a stony bridleway, rising gently across the fields.

5 Ignore turn-offs until you come to **Fox Heads Farm**. Turn left along the track here, passing left of the farmhouse. The dirt and stone track descends to a bridge over a stream, then climbs again past an **old quarry**. Though there are a few climbs the track is still quite easy, being

smooth-surfaced and fairly well drained. Often it's lined with bramble, ferns and foxgloves, with the odd tree. Just beyond the summit of the hill the track bends right. After being joined from the right by another farm track it comes to the road, just to the west of **Sicklinghall village**.

6 Turn left along the road into the village. On the right there's a pond with lilies and coots, then on the left there's another pub, the **Scott Arms**. The winding road makes a long but gradual descent towards Wetherby, passing the upmarket **Linton Springs Hotel**. Beyond the hotel, ignore the right turn 'to Linton'. After passing through housing in the Wetherby suburbs watch out for the **blue cyclists' sign**. This marks the access road back to the car park.

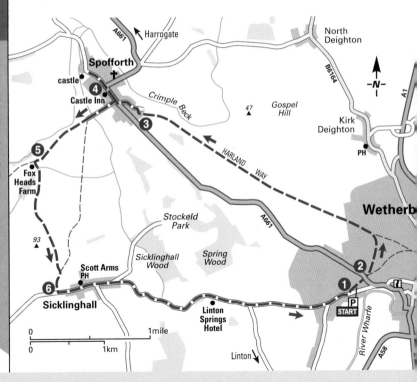

The Castle

Sited on Spofforth's main street, the Castle Inn has old red sandstone walls clad with a little creeping ivy and, in summer, with colourful hanging baskets. There's a courtyard in the back for outdoor dining.

Food
Home-cooked traditional pub food includes ciabatta sandwiches (roast peppers and goat's cheese), omelettes and pasta meals, alongside cod in beer batter, steak and kidney pie, Castle mixed grill and a range of vegetarian dishes.

Family facilities
Children are allowed in the eating areas of the bar. Smaller portions of any main course dishes on the menu are available.

Alternative refreshment stops
The Scott Arms at Sicklinghall.

☛ Where to go from here
The 58-acre (23.5ha) RHS Harlow Carr Botanical Gardens west of Harrogate includes a breathtaking streamside garden, peaceful woodland and arboretum, and a Museum of Gardening (www.rhs.org.uk). In Harrogate, the Royal Pump Room Museum tells the story of Harrogate's heyday as England's European spa (www.harrogate.gov.uk).

about the pub

The Castle
35 High Street, Spofforth
Harrogate, North Yorkshire HG3 1BQ
Tel: 01937 590200

DIRECTIONS: The Castle in Spofforth is on the route and lies on the corner at the top end of High Street, near the junction with Castle Street

PARKING: 24

OPEN: daily; all day

FOOD: no food Monday

BREWERY/COMPANY: Punch Taverns

REAL ALE: Black Sheep Bitter, Ruddles County, Timothy Taylor Landlord

Fairburn Ings and Ledsham

WALK

24

Fairburn

WEST YORKSHIRE

A visit to West Yorkshire's very own 'Lake District', now a bird reserve of national importance.

Fairburn and Ledsham

The coalfields of West Yorkshire were most concentrated in the borough of Wakefield. Towns and villages grew up around the mines. When the industry went into decline, mining communities were hit especially hard and thousands of miners lost their jobs. The death of the industry was emphasised by the conversion of Caphouse Colliery into the National Coal Mining Museum for England.

The spoil heaps that scarred the landscape are going back to nature, a process hastened by tree planting and other reclamation schemes. Opencast workings are being transformed into lakes and wetlands – valuable havens for wildfowl and migrating birds. Within a single generation West and South Yorkshire may have a network of lakes to rival the Norfolk Broads. In the meantime, these industrial wastelands are still rather scruffy.

Fairburn Ings, now under the stewardship of the Royal Society for the Protection of Birds (RSPB), was one of the earliest examples of colliery reclamation – designated a Local Nature Reserve in 1957. The result is arguably the most important nature reserve in West Yorkshire. The stark outlines of the spoil heaps are now softened by banks of silver birches, and mining subsidence has created a broad expanse of water near the village of Fairburn, as well as smaller pools and flashes.

Hidden away from the traffic hammering up and down the nearby A1, the estate village of Ledsham is a tranquil little backwater. Behind the Saxon church – one of the oldest in West Yorkshire – is a row of picturesque almshouses.

the walk

1 Walk down Cut Road as it narrows to a track. Soon you have the main **lake** to your right, and a smaller stretch of water to your left. The track finishes at the end of the lake, on approaching the River Aire.

2 Go right here, to join a path along the top of a ridge (actually an old spoil heap), with the river to your left and the lake right. Beyond the lake the path crosses a broader expanse of spoil heap, through **scrubland**, following the river in a broad arc to the right, before descending to a stile above another small mere. Turn right on a broad track here, then at a double gate, turn left onto a **signed nature trail**. Take the first right, a duckboard path across wetlands and leading to the **information centre**.

3 Go through the **car park** to the road. Go right for 100yds (91m), then go left (signed 'Ledston and Kippax') for just 100yds (91m), and pick up a path on your right that

Taking a path through the trees at Fairburn Ings, an important colliery reclamation

MAP: OS Explorer 289 Leeds
START/FINISH: free parking in Cut Road, Fairburn; grid ref: SE 472278
PATHS: good paths and tracks (some newly created from spoil heaps), 7 stiles
LANDSCAPE: lakes, riverside and reclaimed colliery spoil heaps
PUBLIC TOILETS: Fairburn Ings visitor centre
TOURIST INFORMATION: Leeds, tel 0113 242 5242
THE PUB: Chequers Inn, Ledsham
🛈 Deep water at the Fairburn lakes between points 1 & 2; pub closed Sundays

Getting to the start

Fairburn lies just off the A1 near South Milford. From the dual carriageway exit road, turn right down Gaux Street into the village, then right again. The car park is on the left at the junction with Cut Road. Note: at the time of writing the A1M was under construction and might change the entry system into the village.

Researched and written by:
John Gillham, John Morrison

2h30 — 5 MILES — 8 KM — LEVEL 1 23

24

WALK

Fairburn WEST YORKSHIRE

hugs the right-hand fringe of a **wood**. Beyond the wood, take a path between fields; it broadens to a track as you approach the village of Ledsham. At a new estate of houses, turn right, along **Manor Garth**.

4 You arrive in the village by the **ancient church**. Turn left along the road, past the church to reach the **Chequers Inn**. Retrace your steps through the village, then, where the road bears left, take a gate on the right, giving access to a good track uphill. Where the main track goes right, into fields, continue along a track ahead, into woodland. Leave the wood by a stile, then turn left to trace the woodland's edge.

5 Where the wood ends follow **hedgerow** on the right side of the field, then aim slightly left to locate the stile into a narrow spur of woodland. Beyond this, head

what to look for

Be sure to take a pair of binoculars with you. Fairburn Ings is a bird reserve of national importance and, especially during the spring and autumn migrations, all kinds of rare birds can be seen. There are a number of strategically sited hides along this walk, from which you can watch the birds without disturbing them. Watch especially for the rare but inconspicuous gadwall, pochard and golden plover.

slightly left, uphill, across the next field, to follow a fence and hedgerow. Go through a kissing gate by a **cottage** on the right and follow an enclosed track, past **houses** in the later stages. Go left, when you meet the road, and back into the village of Fairburn.

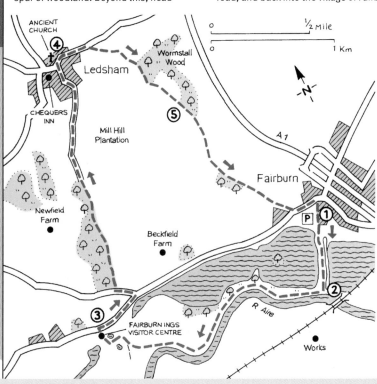

Chequers Inn

Deep in the Don valley at the heart of the hidden estate village stands the old ivy-covered Chequers, with a history that can be traced back to 1540. A popular, thriving local with a low, roadside, bow-fronted window that lends an almost Dickensian air, it has been closed on Sundays for over 170 years due to the one-time lady of the manor being offended by drunken farm workers on her way to church. To avoid this happening in future, she decreed that Sundays in Ledsham should be 'dry'. The pub is still owned by the same family. Inside are low beams, cosy alcoves, log fires, old wooden settles and a bustling, traditional atmosphere. Tiered above a pebbled walkway are the colourful flower-filled patios that form the beer garden, so well frequented in summer.

Food

Popular bar food includes soups, filled baguettes and light meals like tomato and mozzarella salad and king scallops with spinach mayonnaise. Main dishes take in shank of lamb with mustard mash and juniper berry sauce, beef fillet with Madeira sauce, and steak and mushroom pie.

Family facilities

Children are welcome in the eating area of the bar and in the dining room.

Alternative refreshment stops

None on route. Range of options in Castleford and Leeds.

☛ Where to go from here

Temple Newsam Estate on the edge of Leeds is one of the finest Jacobean houses in the

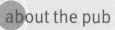

about the pub

Chequers Inn
Claypit Lane, Ledsham
South Milford, West Yorkshire
LS25 5LP
Tel: 01977 683135
www.thechequersinn.f9.co.uk

DIRECTIONS: Ledsham is 1 mile (1.6km) off the A1 at the junction with the A63. Pub is in the village centre.

PARKING: 35

OPEN: daily Monday to Friday; all day Saturday; closed Sunday

FOOD: daily

BREWERY/COMPANY: free house

REAL ALE: Brown Cow Bitter & Simpson's No 4, John Smiths, Timothy Taylor Landlord, Theakston Best

DOGS: allowed in the bar and garden

North of England with stately and historic treasures, a rare breeds farm, walled garden and acres of woodland and parkland (www.leeds.gov.uk/templenewsam). North off the A1 is Lotherton Hall (www.leeds.gov.uk/lothertonhall), an Edwardian house filled with collections of costumes, furniture and oriental art, and there's a deer park and bird garden.

High Ackworth and East Hardwick

An undemanding stroll through history in rolling, pastoral countryside to the east of Wakefield.

Ackworth

With its village green acting as the centre-piece for some fine old houses, High Ackworth has a pleasantly old-fashioned air and is now a designated conservation area. Today the village is best known for its school, founded by a prominent Quaker, John Fothergil, to teach the children of 'Friends not in affluence', in October 1779. Opposite the village green are almshouses, built in 1741 to house 'a schoolmaster and six poor women'. Nearby Ackworth Old Hall, dating from the early 17th century, is said to be haunted by John Nevison, a notorious robber and highwayman. His most famous act of daring was in 1676 when he rode from Rochester to York in just 15 hours. The story goes that he committed a robbery and was afraid he had been recognised. Fleeing the scene, he covered the 230 miles (370km) in record time. When he arrived in York, he asked the Lord Mayor the time. After his arrest he used the Mayor as his alibi and he was acquitted. No one believed the journey could be made in so short a time.

Until the Reformation, the stone plinth on the village green was topped by a cross. It was knocked off by Cromwell's troops. The cross had been erected in memory of Father Thomas Balne of nearby Nostell Priory, who once preached from here. On a pilgrimage to Rome, he succumbed to the plague. When his body was being brought back to the priory, mourners insisted on opening the coffin here in High Ackworth. As a result, the plague devasted the community. The Plague Stone, by the Pontefract Road, dates from a second outbreak in 1645.

the walk

1 From the top of the village green, take a narrow ginnel immediately to the right of **Manor House**. Beyond a stile made of stone slabs (not the last you'll see today), keep to the right-hand edge of a small field, to another stile. A ginnel brings you out into **Woodland Grove**; go left here, then first

right, to meet the A628, Pontefract Road. Go left, but for just 100yds (91m). Look out on the right for a gap in the hedgerow and a footpath sign (opposite a house called **Tall Trees**). Walk straight across a field (follow the direction of the sign), to a tiny footbridge over a beck. Continue along the right-hand edge of the next field, over another tiny bridge. Keep ahead between fields – going sharp left, then sharp right, over another footbridge – to follow a hedgerow. When you come to a gap in the hedge, head straight across the next two fields (towards the **houses** you see ahead).

2 Take a bridge over a railway line, and continue between fields towards **Hundhill Farm**. Keep right at the farm's boundary wall, to a stile. Bear left along the lane; after just 75yds (69m), and after a left-hand bend, take a gap stile in the wall on your right, on to an enclosed path. Beyond the next stile, bear right along a minor road that soon meets the A639. Cross the road, passing the **old village pump**, and walk into the village of **East Hardwick**. Beyond the **church**, where the road bears left, look out for a sign ('Public Bridleway') on your right, just before a house called **Bridleways**.

3 Go right here, along a track between hedgerows. Soon after the track goes left, take a gap in the hedge to your right. Follow a field path uphill, keeping a hedgerow to your right. At the top of this narrow field, keep straight ahead on a footpath between fields. Follow a drainage channel to meet a crossing track. Go right here, to cross over the A639 again. Take the road ahead (this is Rigg Lane) and, at **White Gates Farm**, go left, between farm buildings, on to a concrete track.

| 2h30 | 5 MILES | 8 KM | LEVEL 1 2 3 |

MAP: OS Explorer 278 Sheffield & Barnsley
START/FINISH: High Ackworth, park near church and village green; grid ref: SE 441180
PATHS: mostly field paths; care should be taken with route finding, on the first section to East Hardwick, 11 stiles
LANDSCAPE: gently rolling, arable country
PUBLIC TOILETS: none on route
TOURIST INFORMATION: Wakefield, tel 01924 305000
THE PUB: The Brown Cow, High Ackworth
🛈 Busy and fast roads to cross at High Ackworth and East Hardwick

Getting to the start
High Ackworth is on the A628 road 3 miles south of Pontefract. The village green, where there is parking, can be found to the west of The Brown Cow pub. Coming from the west it is on the left, just beyond the junction with the 'Featherstone' B road.

Researched and written by:
John Gillham, John Morrison

Below: The Plague Stone in High Ackworth recalls the second outbreak here in 1645

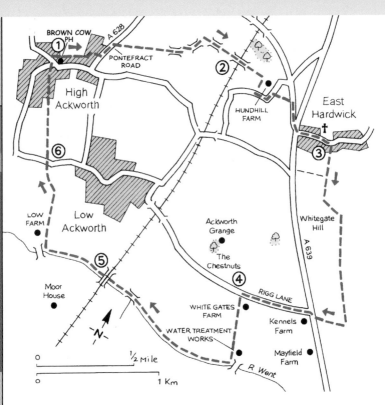

4 Follow this track past a **water treatment works**, to a concrete bridge over the River Went (notice the old packhorse bridge next to it). Without crossing either bridge, bear right, on a field-edge path, to accompany the river. A little **plank bridge** takes you across a side-beck, before you walk beneath the six arches of a railway viaduct.

5 Continue by the riverside, passing (not crossing) a stone bridge over the river. Bear right here, across the corner of a field, in front of the barns of **Low Farm**, to join a field-edge path. Follow a hedge towards houses, to a stile and a road. This is **Low Ackworth**.

6 Cross the road and take a ginnel between houses. Beyond a stile at the far end, bear half left across a field to a stile and across another field. A stile gives

access to another ginnel. Continue along Hill Drive, soon bearing right, down into a **cul-de-sac**. At the bottom, take a narrow ginnel on the left, to arrive back in High Ackworth near the village green and **The Brown Cow**.

what to look for

Village greens are uncommon features in West Yorkshire, a county in which even the smallest community can feel like a town. But the Industrial Revolution passed Ackworth by; no mill chimneys ever disturbed the symmetry. Surrounded by buildings of character – including the parish church, Manor House and a row of almshouses – Ackworth has managed to retain its village atmosphere.

The Brown Cow

about the pub

The Brown Cow
Pontefract Road, Ackworth
Pontefract, West Yorkshire WF7 7EL
Tel: 01977 704735

DIRECTIONS: beside the A628 and village green in High Ackworth	
PARKING: 30	
OPEN: daily; all day Friday, Saturday and Sunday	
FOOD: daily at lunchtime; Thursday, Friday and Saturday evenings only	
BREWERY/COMPANY: Enterprise Inns	
REAL ALE: John Smiths, guest beer	
DOGS: not allowed inside the pub	

On the main road near the triangular village green, this Victorian pub was once a coaching inn. There are a couple of tables in front of the pub and a few more to the rear. A large carpeted bar area with a deep sofa and a combination of upholstered bench seats and wooden cottage-style chairs characterise the plushly refurbished interior.

Food
From the standard menu you can order sandwiches, jacket potatoes, omelettes, lasagne, gammon and chips and a choice of steaks. Daily home-made specials may include spinach and ricotta cannelloni, salmon and broccoli mornay, a roast joint of beef (also used for sandwiches), and chilli with rice.

Family facilities
Children are very welcome in the dining areas if they are eating. There's a kiddies menu and half-portions of some main meals are available.

Alternative refreshment stops
There are restaurants in Ackworth.

☛ Where to go from here
Spend some time at Nostell Priory, built in the mid 18th century and extended in 1766 and containing a notable saloon, a tapestry room, pictures and Chippendale furniture (www.nationaltrust.org.uk). Take the children to the National Coal Mining Museum near Wakefield and travel 460ft (140m) underground for a tour with an ex-miner. Discover the fascinating galleries and exhibitions, explore the colliery site and meet the pit ponies (www.ncm.org.uk). South of Wakefield, off the M1, is the Yorkshire Sculpture Park at West Bretton (www.ysp.co.uk). Set in 500 acres (202ha) of 18th century designed landscape, it is an international centre for modern and contemporary sculpture.

A loop from Swainby to Whorlton

From the once-industrial village of Swainby, a walk with fine views from the Moors and a taste of history in Whorlton.

Swainby and Whorlton

The charming and peaceful village street of Swainby, divided by a tree-lined stream, gives few hints of its dramatic past. It owes its existence to the plague in the 14th century. The inhabitants of the original village, up the hill at Whorlton, deserted their homes and moved here. In the 19th century Swainby was shocked out of its peaceful existence by the opening of the ironstone mines in Scugdale.

Jet was also mined in the Swainby area in the 19th century, including on Whorl Hill, which you will walk around. Most of the jet pits were small but they could be very profitable. The industry had virtually died out by the 1920s.

The path from Whorl Hill takes us into the deserted village of Whorlton. Little survived its abandonment after the plague except the church and the castle, both now partially ruined. A flap in the doorway of the church allows you to see a fine oak figure of a knight, probably Nicholas, Lord Maynell, who fought with Edward I in Wales. The gatehouse of Maynell's castle, just along the road, is the only substantial part left. It was built at the end of the 14th century, and was besieged 250 years later during the Civil War. You can still see the marks of cannon balls from the Parliamentarians' guns on the walls. East of the castle are further earthworks.

Swainby

NORTH YORKSHIRE

the walk

1 With the **church** on your left, walk down the village street to the right of the stream. Continue past a sign 'Unsuitable for Coaches' and straight ahead uphill. As the road bends to the right, follow the bridleway sign to **Scugdale**, up the track ahead.

2 Go through two gates, turning left after the second into the woods to join the waymarks for the **Cleveland Way National Trail**. Walk through the woodland, turning left, at an opening, down to a stile. The footpath goes downhill across the fields to another gate. Cross the **stream** on the footbridge then turn left along a lane, with another footbridge, over **Scugdale Beck**.

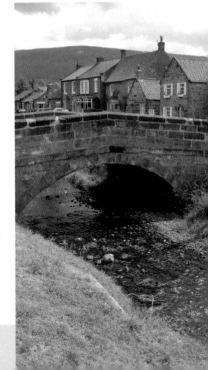

The remains of 14th-century Whorlton Castle

WALK

2h30	6 MILES	9.7 KM	LEVEL 1 2 3

MAP: OS Explorer OL26 North York Moors – Western

START/FINISH: roadside parking in Swainby village; grid ref: NZ 477020

PATHS: tracks and moorland paths, lots of bracken, 11 stiles

LANDSCAPE: farmland and moorland, with some woodland

PUBLIC TOILETS: none on route

TOURIST INFORMATION: Guisborough, tel 01287 633801

THE PUB: The Black Horse, Swainby

🛈 Route finding could be difficult when the mists come down over the moors – save this route for settled weather

Swainby

NORTH YORKSHIRE

Getting to the start

Swainby lies just off the busy A172 Teesside road 5 miles (8km) beyond the junction with the A19 and 12 miles (19.3km) due south of Middlesbrough. Turn south down the village street alongside the stream and park by the church. The Blacksmith's Arms lies on the corner at the north end of this street.

Researched and written by:
John Gillham, David Winpenny

3 Follow the lane past **Hollin Hill Farm** to a T-junction with telephone and post boxes. Cross the lane and go through a Cleveland Way signed gate. Walk up the path beside woodland to a **gate** (there's a view of the valley from this ridge).

4 The path turns right to a gate and goes on to a paved track in the wood. Go straight ahead at a crossing track to another gate, and continue to follow the paved path on to the **heather moorland**. After the first summit, the path descends beyond a **cairn** into a dip. After the paved path ends, look out for a very narrow path off to the left, down through the heather.

5 After about 100yds (91m) you will reach a **concrete post** where the path forks. Take the left fork and follow the path down the gully to a fence beside a wall. Turn left, forking left again down another gully to a signpost by a wall and fence. Follow the sign left and go over a **spoil heap** to reach a gate on your right.

6 Through the gate, go straight down the hill through woodland. At the bottom cross a track to a stile by a gate and go down the lane. Just past some **houses**,

The beck flowing through the village of Swainby on the North York Moors

where **Whorl Hill Wood** begins, take a footpath over two stiles and climb alongside the inside edge of the wood.

7 The track bends right with the perimeter of the wood and levels out. At a T-junction, turn left and follow the track downhill to a stile and out of the woods. Go straight ahead through a **gateway** and follow a grassy track beside the **farmhouse**.

8 Go over a stile beside a gate and follow the track along the hillside. Over a stile with steps beyond, turn left at the bottom and follow the field edge. Go over a **waymarked stile** by a gate and along the field. Walk along the field to a gate at the end, then follow the metalled lane past **Whorlton church** and **castle** back to Swainby village. To get to the Black Horse, turn right along the lane that traces the nearside bank of the stream.

what to look for

From the highest part of the walk, which takes you up on to the northern edge of the North York Moors plateau, you are rewarded with extensive northward views over the vast industrial complexes surrounding Middlesbrough. It was the production of iron from the hills which really put Middlesbrough on the map; it had a population of just 40 in 1829, 7,600 in 1851, when the first blast furnace opened, and 20,000 nine years later. Prime Minister Gladstone called the town 'an infant Hercules'. Beyond the River Tees, the area of Seal Sands is home to an oil refinery and chemical works. It's the terminal of the 220 mile (352km) pipeline bringing oil and gas from the Ekofisk field in the North Sea. If you are on the hills at dawn or dusk, you may see the flare stacks glowing on the skyline.

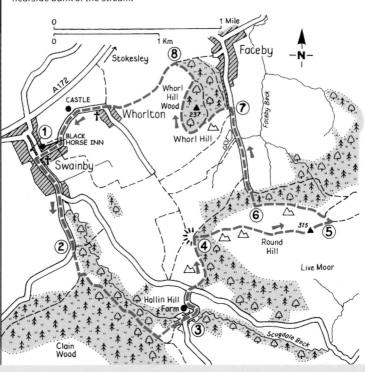

The Black Horse

The Black Horse is an attractive stone-
and brick-built pub with traditional
North York Moors red-tiled roof. It's in
a quiet location, overlooking the small
stream and green that dissect the whole
of the village. The Black Horse is a very
friendly and informal local serving
tasty dishes.

Food

The extensive menu offers pasta meals,
sizzling skillets, traditional meat dishes
like steak and ale pie, loin of lamb with
redcurrant and mint sauce and beef
Wellington, as well as numerous fish
dishes. Lighter lunchtime meals include a
sandwich selection. There's a popular
Sunday lunch menu with four roasts.

Family facilities

Children are very welcome in the pub
and there's a separate menu for younger
children. Large playing field to the rear
of the pub.

about the pub

The Black Horse
23 High Street, Swainby
Northallerton, North Yorkshire
DL6 3ED
Tel: 01642 700436

DIRECTIONS: see Getting to the start	
PARKING: 50	
OPEN: daily; all day Sunday	
FOOD: daily; all day Sunday	
BREWERY/COMPANY: Pubmaster	
REAL ALE: Cameron's Strongarm, John Smiths	
DOGS: allowed in the garden only	

Alternative refreshment stops

Also in Swainsby is the Blacksmiths Arms.

☛ Where to go from here

Spend a moment of solitude at nearby
Mount Grace Priory (www.english-
heritage.org.uk), the best preserved of
England's charterhouses – communities of
Carthusian monks. There's a reconstructed
monk's cell showing how they lived as
hermits, coming together
rarely except for services in
the church. Learn about
Captain Cook's early life
and education at the
Captain Cook Schoolroom
Museum in Great Ayton
(www.captaincookschool
roommuseum.co.uk).

Swainby

NORTH YORKSHIRE

Bardsey and Pompocali

A rolling landscape with
Roman echoes.

Roman connections

The Romans built a network of important
roads across Yorkshire linking their most
important forts. One of these roads passed
close to Bardsey village and you walk a
short stretch of the old Roman road when
you take the track from Hetchell Wood.
Adjacent to these woods – and marked on

the Ordnance Survey map as Pompocali –
are a set of intriguing earthworks. Though
rather overgrown, they are unencumbered
by signs and information panels. Roman
finds have been unearthed here. A couple
of miles away, at Dalton Parlours, the site of
a large Roman villa has been discovered.

Once the Romans had abandoned this
outpost, Bardsey became part of the
kingdom of Elmet, and was later mentioned
in the Domesday Book. By the 13th century,
the village had been given to the monks of

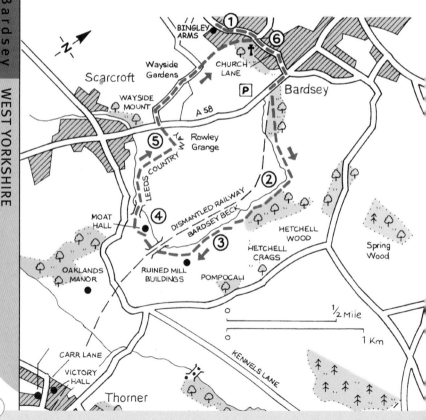

A rural view beyond the commuter village of Bardsey

Kirkstall Abbey. After the dissolution of the monasteries, in 1539, Bardsey came under the control of powerful local families. The Parish Church of All Hallows, visited near the end of this walk, is another antiquity – the core of the building is Anglo Saxon.

Above the church is a grassy mound, where a castle once stood. From pottery found on the site, archaeologists can tell it was occupied during the 12th and 13th centuries, after which it was abandoned.

Close to the city, yet retaining its own identity, Bardsey has expanded beyond its ancient centre and is a commuter village for people who work in Leeds. The Bingley Arms pub can claim a long existence; there is documentary evidence of brewers and innkeepers going back a thousand years. Bardsey is, in short, a historic little spot.

the walk

1 With your back to the Bingley Arms turn right along **Church Lane** to the T-junction with the A58 Wetherby Road. Turn right here, then after about 200yds (183m) turn left past some **metal bollards** into the woods. Join the old **railway trackbed**, going right, for just a few paces, before bearing left, over a stile, to continue on a woodland path. After passing through a narrow meadow on a field-edge path, continue with a fence to your left and the woods to your right. Keep straight ahead when the fence ends to enter a huge field. Ignore the path across the field ahead but instead turn right, following a hedge and **Bardsey Beck**, downhill.

| 2h00 | 3.5 MILES | 5.7 KM | LEVEL 1 23 |

WALK

MAP: OS Explorer 289 Leeds

START/FINISH: Roadside parking on Church Lane in Bardsey; grid ref: SE 369430

PATHS: good paths and tracks (though some, being bridleways, may be muddy), 8 stiles

LANDSCAPE: arable and woodland

PUBLIC TOILETS: none on route

TOURIST INFORMATION: Leeds, tel 0113 242 5242

THE PUB: The Bingley Arms, Bardsey

🅛 Busy road through Bardsey and a dangerous road crossing at point 5. Unattended young children could wander off the slippery river bank in a couple of places between Points 2 and 3

Getting to the start

Bardsey is located just west of the A58 between Leeds and Wetherby. From Wetherby, turn right into the village along Church Lane, where there is parking and The Bingley Arms.

Researched and written by:
John Gillham, John Morrison

Bardsey

WEST YORKSHIRE

2 Through an opening, you enter **Hetchell Wood**. Keep right, on a good path through the woods, soon passing beneath **Hetchell Crags**, whose soft gritstone façade offers a challenge to local climbers. You soon come to a meeting of paths, close to a wooden footbridge over the beck. Don't cross the beck, but go left for a few paces and along a track (of Roman origin) going uphill.

3 Go right, almost immediately, over a stile. The path goes right, around the **earthworks** (marked on the map as Pompocali), but first you should take five minutes to investigate these intriguing remains. Pass between a stream and an over-hanging rock; take a stile next to a gate. Walk uphill to pass **ruinous mill buildings**, take another stile, and join a good track that takes you under the old railway line. Immediately after crossing a stream, go through a small gate on the right and walk diagonally left across a small field to another gate where you turn right along a lane. Beyond the main gate to **Moat Hall**, follow a track for just 20yds (18m), and take a step stile in the wall on your right.

4 Take a field-edge path, with a hedge to the right (from here back to Bardsey you are walking the Leeds Country Way). Towards the far end of the field your path bears right into a copse. Cross a stile and a

Walking near Bardsey

beck on a little wooden footbridge. Go left, as you leave the copse, and immediately left again on to a hollow way hemmed in by hedgerows. Follow this path through scrubland, past a couple of small **fishing lakes**, to emerge at a field. Continue up a field-edge path, keeping a hedge to your right. At the top of the hill, walk downhill for 75yds (69m). Where the hedge ends you meet a cross-track. Ignore the good track ahead and go left here on a track that follows a wall to meet the A58 road.

5 Walk left for just 20yds (18m) and bear right on to **Wayside Mount**, an unsurfaced access road that serves a collection of detached houses. Beyond the last **house** go through a gate and follow the track ahead, with a tall hedge on your left. When the track bears left walk ahead down a field-edge path, following a hedge on the left. Bear half right, near the bottom of the field, to join a narrow path through scrubland, over a little beck, and up to a gate into the **churchyard**. Keep right of the church to meet a road.

6 Go right on Church Lane back to your car, or left if you're going straight to The Bingley Arms.

The Bingley Arms

The Guinness Book of Records *lists the Bingley Arms as the oldest inhabited inn and brewhouse in England with records dating back to AD 905. Formerly known as the Priests Inn, it was once connected with Kirkstall Abbey and was used as a rest house for travelling monks. The impressive stone building is partially clad with ivy and shaded by a fine willow tree. Inside it is crammed with historical interest with an old-world atmosphere created by exposed wooden beams, wood-panelled walls hung with hunting prints, cushioned settles and open log fires. Don't miss a glimpse of the beautiful upstairs dining hall. A lovely terraced garden filled with flowers makes a delightful place to sit on warm summer days.*

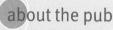

about the pub

The Bingley Arms
37 Church Lane
Bardsey, Leeds,
West Yorkshire LS17 9DR
Tel: 01937 572462

DIRECTIONS: see Getting to the Start; the pub is on Church lane	
PARKING: 70	
OPEN: daily; all day	
FOOD: all day Sunday; no food Sunday evening and Monday	
BREWERY/COMPANY: Honeycombe Leisure	
REAL ALE: Timothy Taylor Landlord, Moorhouses Black Cat, Black Sheep Bitter, Tetley	
DOGS: allowed in taproom and garden on leads	

Food

Expect a good choice of interesting bar meals ranging from the traditional – steak and mushroom pie, lambs' liver and bacon and pork sausages on creamy mash – to home-made curries, Chinese dishes and pasta meals. Good steaks, daily specials and a popular sandwich menu.

Family facilities

Children are welcome in all areas of the pub and half portions of all the dishes on the bar menu are available.

Alternative refreshment stops

None on route. There are other refreshment opportunities in Bardsey.

☛ Where to go from here

At nearby Bramham Park you will find a splendid Queen Anne mansion built in 1698. The beautiful gardens were laid out by Robert Benson, 1st Lord Bingley, with cascades, ponds and grand vistas in the manner of Versailles (www.bramhampark.co.uk). In Roundhay Park on the northern edge of Leeds you will find Tropical World. Here the atmosphere of the tropics is recreated with exotic trees, waterfall cascades, a Nocturnal House, a South American rainforest, and a Desert House (www.vrleeds.co.uk).

The Hambleton Hills

An exciting ride on the top of the moors.

Hambleton Hills

The long tarmac lane that takes you north from Sutton Bank seems unremarkable in itself, but there's a history, dating back to the Iron Age tribes who settled here around 400BC. They would have used this road long before the Romans followed in their footsteps. Evidence of the tribes' existence is all around you, from the burial tumuli near the escarpment's edge to a 60 acre (24.3ha) fort on Roulston Scar. Strangely, there are no traces of any hut circles within the fort's huge ramparts. It is possible that this was a temporary bastion in times of war, but it could also have been a huge cattle corral for neighbouring settlements.

Hambleton has many connections with beasts of burden. When the Great North Road became a turnpike the Scottish cattle drovers turned to the hills to avoid the tolls. The previously mentioned road became known as the Hambleton Drove Road, a busy highway with several drovers' inns along the way. Hereabouts there were two – one, Dialstone House, is now a farm, but the other, the Hambleton Hotel, remains an inn.

Hambleton has long been associated with racehorses. In 1740 an Act of Parliament decreed that racing could only take place at Hambleton, York and Newmarket. Fifteen years later, however, the racecourse was closed, but nearby Hambleton House is to this day a well-known training stable for thoroughbreds.

the ride

1 Before you leave the centre, take a look at the panoramas to the south and west, for you can see for miles across the flat fields of the Vales of Mowbray and York. Alf Wight, alias the fictional vet James Herriot, believed this view to be the finest in England. Apparently, both York Minster and Lincoln Cathedral are discernible on a clear day. From the visitor centre car park, turn left up

| 2h00 | 7.4 MILES | 12 KM | LEVEL 2 3 |

the lane signed to Cold Kirby and Old Byland. Take the left fork past **Dialstone Farm** and its tall **communications mast**, before heading north on an ever-so-straight lane through cornfields and pastures.

2 The lane comes to a T-junction by a triangular wood, the **Snack Yate Plantation**. This is a popular starting point for serious mountain bikers who will swoop down on rough tracks through Boltby Forest. Your route turns left down the lane. It's a gentle downhill for a short distance. Just before the road dives off the edge, turn left through a gate on to a grassy bridleway along the escarpment's edge. You're riding on the Hambleton Hills. The first stretch is slightly uphill, but the track is firm and the views wide-sweeping. You'll see a small **reservoir** surrounded by forestry and the village of **Boltby** huddled under a pastured hill.

3 The bridleway climbs to the top of the hill at **High Barn**, an old stone ruin shaded by a fine stand of sycamore. The going eases and the cliffs of an **old quarry** appear ahead. Here the bridleway goes through a gate on to a walled track for a short way. Ignore the bridleway on the left, which goes back to the Hambleton Road, and stay with the edge path to the hill above the rocks of **Boltby Scar**. This is the highest point of the ride. Note the wind-warped larch trees around here – they add to the views over the edge and across the expansive Vale of Mowbray.

4 The trees of the **Boltby Forest** now cover the west slopes, almost to the summit.

A view near Boltby Forest

MAP: OS Explorer OL26 North York Moors – Western

START/FINISH: Sutton Bank Visitor Centre; grid ref: SE 516831

TRAILS/TRACKS: good level lanes followed by undulating bridleways on the escarpment's edge

LANDSCAPE: pastoral plateau and moorland ridge

PUBLIC TOILETS: Sutton Bank Visitor Centre

TOURIST INFORMATION: Sutton Bank Visitor Centre, tel 01845 597426 (weekends only Jan– Feb)

CYCLE HIRE: none locally

THE PUB: The Hambleton Inn, Sutton Bank

🛈 A short section near Point 5 becomes narrower and with a few rocks in places. Inexperienced cyclists should dismount

Getting to the start

Sutton Bank is 6 miles (9.7km) east of Thirsk. Take the A170 Scarborough turn-off from the A19 at Thirsk. This climbs the difficult road to Sutton Bank (caravans prohibited). The centre and car park are on the left at the top.

Why do this cycle ride?

You can enjoy some of the north of England's best views and experience a bit of adventure with a ride on the 'edge'.

Researched and written by: John Gillham

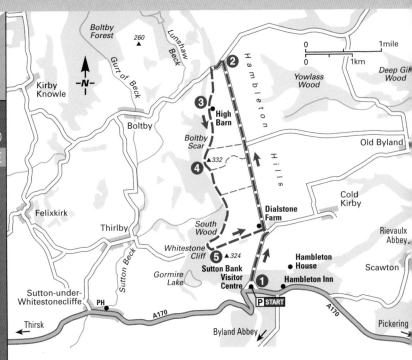

Beyond the next offshoot bridleway, which you should ignore, the path becomes narrower with a few embedded rocks in places. The difficulties are short-lived, but the younger and less experienced riders might prefer to dismount. The riding gets easier again as the bridleway arcs right above **South Wood**. At the end of this arc you turn left to a sign that tells you that the continuing edge path is for walkers only. This is a fine spot to linger and admire the views. To the south the half-moon-shaped **Gormire Lake** lies in a nest of broad-leaved woodland and beneath the sandy-coloured **Whitestone Cliff**.

5 When you've rested, turn left on a bridleway to **Dialstone Farm**. This heads east across large prairie-like fields. Beyond a wood, the **High Quarry Plantation**, you'll see the hurdles of the **equestrian centre**.

A cyclist takes a track near Boltby Forest

Past the large **farm** turn right along the tarred lane, then right again, back to the visitor centre car park.

The Hambleton Inn

about the pub

The Hambleton Inn
Sutton Bank, Thirsk
North Yorkshire YO7 2HA
Tel: 01845 597202

DIRECTIONS: beside the A170 Thirsk to Scarborough road, at the top of Sutton Bank	
PARKING: 50	
OPEN: all day Sunday; closed Monday except Bank Holidays	
FOOD: daily; all day Sunday	
BREWERY/COMPANY: free house	
REAL ALE: local Hambleton ales	

Just a few hundred yards from the Sutton Bank edge and those famous James Herriot views, The Hambleton Inn is backed up by sprucewoods. It's an extremely popular pub with walkers and cyclists. The whitewashed Georgian building was once frequented by cattle drovers, who herded their beasts across the high Hambleton Drove Road. The inn has a large lawned garden to the rear, and flagged patios to the front and sides. Expect an enthusiastic and extremely friendly service, imaginative pub food, summer hog roasts and live entertainment.

Food
Food is freshly prepared and a cut above the pub norm. Snacks include a traditional ploughman's lunch and baked baguettes (crab and lemon mayonnaise, roast ham and pickle), while more substantial bar meals range from beef burger and chips and deep-fried Whitby haddock and chips to liver and bacon with onion gravy, and pasta with poached salmon and lemon and watercress sauce. Separate evening menu.

Family facilities
The pub is really geared up for families. Children are very welcome inside the pub where an above-average children's menu is available for younger family members, as well as smaller portions of adult dishes. When the weather's fine there's good patio seating and a large lawned area with play area to keep children amused.

Alternative refreshment stops
Café at Sutton Bank Visitor Centre.

☛ Where to go from here
Visit nearby Rievaulx Abbey (www.english-heritage.org.uk), once the most important Cistercian abbey in Britain; the soaring ruins are powerfully atmospheric in the beautiful Rye valley. Another evocative ruin to explore is Byland Abbey at the base of the Hambleton Hills, or head east to Pickering to take a steam railway journey through stunning scenery on the North Yorkshire Moors Railway (www.northyorkshiremoorsrailway.com).

Byland Abbey and Oldstead Observatory

From the romantic ruins of Byland Abbey to an old observatory – and back through the fish pond.

Byland Abbey

In 1134 a party of Savigniac monks set out from their English mother house in Furness on the west coast of Cumbria to found a new monastery. Six moves and 43 years later, Byland was founded as their permanent home, and by then they had become part of the Cistercian Order. The final move was from nearby Stocking, where they had settled in 1147. The relocation to Byland in 1177 must have been long planned, for Byland's earliest buildings, the lay brothers' quarters, were complete by 1165; everything had to be in order for the arrival of the monks themselves.

The most impressive parts of the ruins remaining today are in the church – and especially the remnants of the fine rose window in the west front. Beneath the main door leads into the nave, the lay brothers' portion of the church. Although the walls of the south transept collapsed in 1822, that area of the church still retains one of Byland's greatest treasures – the geometrically tiled floors, with their delicate patterns in red, cream and black.

At the highest point of the walk is Oldstead Observatory, built on the splendidly named Mount Snever by John Wormald, who lived at Oldstead Hall in the valley below. At just over 40ft (12m) high, 1,146ft (349m) above sea level, it is high enough to scan the heavens. History does not record if Mr Wormald made any startling astronomical discoveries.

The ruins of Byland Abbey, dating from 1177

the walk

1 From the car park, walk towards the abbey ruins, then turn left along the lane at the abbey's north side. At a public footpath sign, go left up the drive of **Abbey House**, then right through a waymarked gate just before the house. After a second gateway bear slightly left, skirting a grassy bank towards the top left-hand corner of the field. Here you go though a waymarked gate behind a **bench seat**. Go through two more gates and on to a tarred lane just to the left of the buildings of **Wass** village.

2 Turn left. At a T-junction go through a gate signed **'Cam Farm, Observatory'**. The path climbs then leaves the wood edge to rise to a terrace. After a stile take the left-hand path, signed **Cam Farm**, to join a track climbing uphill to reach a **forestry vehicle turning circle**.

3 Turn right and, just before a waymarked metal gate at the edge of the forest, turn left along the inside wood edge (not waymarked). Follow the path, which soon bends left over wet ground to **Oldstead Observatory**. Pass to the left of the observatory and go down a slope to a track running steeply downhill. The path can be slippery – take care!

4 Turn right along a track, signed **'Oldstead'**, then take a left turn at the next junction, over a stream where it is joined by another track and becomes a tarred country lane. Turn left at the T-junction to pass through Olstead village. Just before the 'road narrows' sign, turn left.

5 Go through some gateposts and over a **cattle grid**. Then, as the avenue of trees ends, take a waymarked footpath to the

Walkers taking a road near Byland Abbey

2h30 – **5 MILES** – **8 KM** – **LEVEL 2**

MAP: OS Explorer OL26 North York Moors – Western

START/FINISH: car park behind Abbey Inn in Byland Abbey; grid ref: SE 548789

PATHS: woodland tracks, field paths, 11 stiles

LANDSCAPE: undulating pasture and woodland on slopes of Hambleton Hills

PUBLIC TOILETS: at Byland Abbey

TOURIST INFORMATION: Sutton Bank Visitor Centre, tel 01845 597426 (weekends only Jan–Feb)

THE PUB: The Abbey Inn, Byland Abbey

ⓘ In summer some paths may be choked with nettles and giant hogweed, so unsuitable for small children

Getting to the start

Byland Abbey is 2 miles (3.2km) south of the A170 road halfway between Thirsk and Helmsley. It is best reached by turning south off the A170 3 miles (4.8km) east of Sutton Bank. In the village turn right by the inn to access the signed car park.

Researched and written by:
John Gillham, David Winpenny

WALK

Byland Abbey

NORTH YORKSHIRE

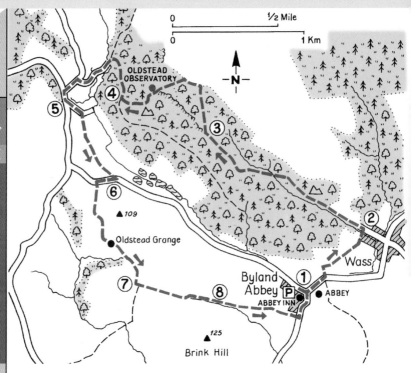

right, uphill to a stile, before climbing a
steep grassy bank. Note: this path can
become overgrown with nettles, bramble
and giant hogweed.

what to look for

The lumps and bumps of the final
field you cross on the walk are the
remains of the monks' ponds. It is difficult to
visualise the abbey in the Middle Ages almost
surrounded by water. There was a large pond that
stretched almost 0.5 mile (800m) from east to
west, to the north of the abbey buildings, which
was used to flush the drains, and two more south
and south east. To the south west, where this
walk passes through, was a roughly triangular
pond, bounded by a bank supporting the abbey's
mill. The ponds were also used for breeding fish,
one of the most important staples of the monks'
diet. They practised large-scale fish farming at
nearby Oldstead Grange.

6 On reaching a tarred lane turn right,
then take a track to the left by the
Oldstead Grange sign. As you near the
house, turn left towards some barns and
wind your way through the **farmyard** to a
stile by a metal gate. Bear half-right
downhill on the track, then bend slightly
right to a waymarked stile.

7 Ten yards/metres beyond the stile turn
left and go through a wood to a **Byland
Abbey signpost**. Follow the path as it
leaves the woods and bends left beyond
Cams Head Farm. Follow the hedge on the
left, before going through a large gap. Now
keep the hedge to the right.

8 The path crosses more fields with
Byland Abbey directly ahead. In the last
field veer left to follow the fence to a
roadside stile. Turn left along the lane, then
left again past the Abbey Inn to the car park.

The Abbey Inn

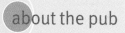
about the pub

The Abbey Inn
Byland Abbey, Coxwold
Thirsk, North Yorkshire YO61 4BD
Tel: 01347 868204
www.bylandabbeyinn.com

DIRECTIONS: see Getting to the Start; pub opposite the abbey ruins

PARKING: 40

OPEN: closed Sunday evening and Monday lunchtime

FOOD: daily

BREWERY/COMPANY: free house

REAL ALE: Black Sheep Bitter, Tetley

DOGS: not allowed inside

ROOMS: 3 en suite

Do seek out this isolated rural pub – it's worth it for the modern British-based food it serves and, if you're looking for somewhere to stay, its superior accommodation. A well-proportioned, creeper-clad façade conceals a highly distinctive interior. The four splendid dining areas have, variously, bare boards, rug-strewn flagstones, open fireplaces, huge settles with scatter cushions, Jacobean-style chairs, and oak and stripped deal tables. Fine tapestries, stuffed birds and unusual objets d'art complete the picture. The abbey ruins are floodlit at night and look amazing from two of the three superb en suite bedrooms. The third overlooks the gardens and surrounding countryside.

Food

Expect a changing menu and daily specials board. At lunchtime your meal could be Brie and red onion tart, chicken and mushroom pie, deep-fried cod with minted pea puree, sweet potato and watercress cakes with chilli dressing, sandwiches, or ploughman's terrine with honey and sunflower bread. Excellent, more elaborate evening menu.

Family facilities

Children of all ages are welcome inside and smaller portions of the main menu dishes are available. Safe large garden for summer eating and drinking. No children overnight.

Alternative refreshment stops

The Wombwell Arms at Wass has bistro-style food, with sandwiches and ploughman's at lunchtime.

☞ Where to go from here

Take a trip to nearby Kilburn to visit the Mouseman Visitor Centre. Here Robert Thompson worked at his now-famous furniture (www.robertthompsons.co.uk). Visit Newburgh Priory, Shandy Hall in Coxwold or the World of James Herriot Museum and Visitor Centre in Thirsk.

York's solar cycle path

A railway track with space in mind and a visit to one of England's most historic cities.

The Railway

York is a railway city so what better way to approach it than on an old railway line. And this old railway line was a famous one – part of the London King's Cross to Edinburgh East Coast Line. Here the *Flying Scotsman* and the world's fastest steam engine, the *Mallard*, thundered along the tracks carrying long trains of dark-red carriages.

So why did they close this stretch? Well, in the early 1980s an ultramodern coalfield at Selby was developed, necessitating a diversion of the railway to avoid the risk of subsidence. Sustrans bought the old line and set about their first major project – a new cycle track, from Riccall to York.

For budding astronomers the line includes a 6.4-mile (10km) scale model of the Solar System, with the Sun being closest to York and Pluto sited near Riccall. Perhaps one of the most fascinating aspects is the Naburn Swing Bridge spanning the River Ouse. Sad and dowdy, its old grey metal structure is showing its age, but there's a fascinating sculpture set across the top. 'The Fisher of Dreams' by Pete Rogers shows an angler sitting peacefully astride the bridge-top with his faithful dog. As you pass below, look closer at that naughty hound, for he is waiting to pee on your bike.

the ride

1 Follow the narrow dirt path leading down to the main trackbed where you turn right. The cycling is easy on a fairly level firm surface. After passing beneath the bridge at **Maude Ridding** and **Naburn Wood** you come to the first planet en route – Uranus. The **church spire** you can see at ten to the hour is that of Naburn village, and soon you pass under the bridge carrying Moor Lane, the Naburn road. Some woods largely obscure the village as you get closer but if you want to visit the village it can be accessed on the left by the **Howden Bridge**, where you see the ringed Saturn model.

2 Just a short way further along the track you reach **Naburn Bridge,** a huge steel structure that carries the track over the River Ouse and its marina. The bridge looks a little neglected, except for the **sculptures** topping it (see 'The Railway'), but it does offer fine views of the tree-lined Ouse, its boats and the vast plains of York. Over the bridge the track continues into the suburb of **Bishopsthorpe** where planet Jupiter awaits.

3 Suddenly there's a sign saying end of the railway track and you find yourself on a **housing estate** without having seen Earth. Don't worry – follow the blue and white cycleway signs first to the right, then left, and you'll soon be back on a tarred track passing Mars, Earth, Venus and Mercury in quick succession.

4 The track passes under the **York Ring Road**. On the other side there's a huge golden globe representing the Sun. Here

| 4h00 | 14 MILES | 22.6 KM | LEVEL 1 2 3 |

the path splits. This is a logical finishing point for those with young children, who will retrace their route back to Escrick. Otherwise, turn right following the tarred track running parallel to the ring road before skirting several fields. The main stand of **York Racecourse** comes into view and the path rounds it to the right, crossing two straights before turning left towards the right side of the **stand**.

5 The path comes to a road just south of the famous **Terry's chocolate factory**, which is about to be shut down. Cross the road at the nearby crossing, turn left along the cycle/walkway, then right on a tarred track descending to the banks of the River Ouse. Turn left along the **riverside promenade**. You'll soon see the ultramodern **Millennium Bridge**. Past **Rowntree Park** and a campsite you follow a quiet back street, Terry Avenue, which still follows the riverside towards the centre of York. Now you'll see the large red and white **pleasure boats** cruising the river.

6 A block of buildings now separates the road from the river. Shortly, at the **Cock and Bottle pub**, turn right back to the riverside, where you should turn left. There are some **cycle racks** by the Ouse Bridge. On the opposite side of the river you'll see the whitewashed **Kings Arms**. To get to it just climb the steps ahead, turn right over the bridge and down the other side; or you could look around the city first. The Railway Museum, the Minster and the Shambles are a must. Retrace your route back along the railway path to Escrick.

Wheeling along the York–Selby cycle track

MAP: OS Explorer 290 York

START/FINISH: Escrick; grid ref: SE 616419

TRAILS/TRACKS: easy-riding former rail track plus back roads

LANDSCAPE: field, suburb and city

PUBLIC TOILETS: none on route

TOURIST INFORMATION: York, tel 01904 621756

CYCLE HIRE: Europcar Cycle Hire, Platform 1, York Station, tel 01904 656161

THE PUB: Kings Arms, Kings Staithe, York

🛈 The route crosses a road and mixes with light traffic from Point 5 (Terry's factory) to the centre of York

Getting to the start

Escrick is just off the A19, 7 miles (11.3km) south east of York. From the north take the A19 turn-off from the A64 ring road, then half a mile (800m) beyond Escrick take the first turn on the right. Turn left at the nearside of the brick-built railway bridge following a rough stone track down to the car park. From the south follow the A19 to York (junction 34 from the M62) and turn left just short of Escrick.

Why do this cycle ride?

If you're new to cycling this is one of the easier routes with smooth surfaces and little traffic, even in the centre of York. The railway verges are flower-filled in spring and summer and the views are superb for most of the way.

Researched and written by: John Gillham

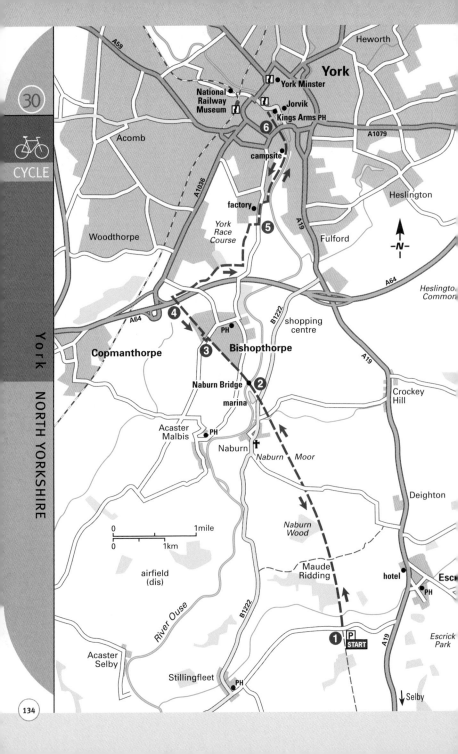

CYCLE

York NORTH YORKSHIRE

Heworth

A59

York

National
Railway
Museum

York Minster

Jorvik
Kings Arms PH

6

Acomb

A1079

campsite

Heslington

factory

York
Race
Course

5

A19

Fulford

A1036

Woodthorpe

A64

Heslingto
Common

4

A64

PH

shopping
centre

B1222

Copmanthorpe

3

Bishopthorpe

A19

Naburn Bridge

2

Crockey
Hill

marina

Acaster
Malbis

PH

Naburn

✝

Naburn Moor

Deighton

Naburn
Wood

0   1mile
0   1km

airfield
(dis)

Maude
Ridding

hotel

Esc

PH

River Ouse

B1222

1

P
START

A19

Escrick
Park

Acaster
Selby

Stillingfleet

PH

↓Selby

Kings Arms

York's most famous pub, is sited right by the river. Each time the Ouse bursts its banks TV cameramen flock to the Kings Arms to capture the floodwaters flowing through the bar – there's a marker by the door that shows the level of famous floods of the past. For that reason, the pub's interior furnishings are spartan. It's a joy, however, to dine on their outside tables, which are laid across a cobbled area, right by the river. The food is simple, but oh-so-tasty alfresco style!

about the pub
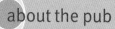

Kings Arms
Kings Staithe, York,
North Yorkshire Yo1 9SN
Tel 01904 659435

DIRECTIONS: Kings Staithe is on the opposite bank of the river to the ride's finishing point	
PARKING: none	
OPEN: daily; all day	
FOOD: no food Sunday evening	
BREWERY/COMPANY: Samuel Smiths	
REAL ALE: none	

Food
Traditional pub food comes in the form of giant Yorkshire puddings filled with tuna or chilli, home-made steak pie, burgers, cheese ploughman's lunch, haddock and chips, a daily roast, and chalkboard specials.

Family facilities
Children are welcome and the pub provides a simple menu for youngsters to choose from. The cobbled riverside area offers a most attractive venue for alfresco dining but children need to be supervised at all times.

Alternative refreshment stops
Though there's nothing en route, there's a wide choice of cafés and pubs in the city.

☛ Where to go from here
While you're in York a visit to the fine minster is a must, as is Jorvik (www.vikingjorvik.com) where you discover what life was like in Viking-age Yorkshire. At the National Railway Museum (www.nrm.org.uk), you will see trains that steamed along the track you've just been on, including the pale-blue streamlined Mallard.

Terrington and Castle Howard

CYCLE

Terrington

NORTH YORKSHIRE

A ride through Yorkshire's most magnificent estate.

Castle Howard

Six years after Henderskelfe Castle burned down in 1693, Charles Howard, the 3rd Earl of Carlisle, asked his friend, Sir John Vanbrugh, to design its replacement, Castle Howard. Vanbrugh at this time was a complete novice, though he would later design Blenheim Palace. However, he formed a successful team with Christopher Wren's clerk, Nicholas Hawksmoor. The building programme would last 100 years, the lifetime of three earls, but the legacy left Yorkshire with one of Britain's most elegant palaces, set among magnificent and colourful gardens, complete with lakes, fountains, classical statues and temples.

In the house itself, the marble entrance hall is lit subtly by a dome. Explore further and you'll see treasures built up over

centuries, including antique sculptures, fine porcelain, and paintings by Rubens, Reynolds and Gainsborough. In 1940 fire came to haunt the Howards once more. A devastating blaze destroyed the dome and twenty of the rooms, leaving the palace open to the elements and in need of extremely costly renovation. That it was done so successfully is all down to George Howard, who inherited the estate after the death of his two brothers in World War Two.

the ride

1 Terrington is a peaceful little village with fine sloping greens either side of the main street, giving the place a spacious feel. The cottages, which are largely Victorian, are built with local limestone. Above them, just off the main street, stands the church, a square-towered building that dates back to Saxon times – there's an

Castle Howard is set amongst 1,000 acres (405ha) of grounds and gardens

Anglo-Saxon window in the south aisle. Much of the structure is 13th-century but was modernised around 1860.

Heading east past the ivy-clad **Bay Horse Inn** towards Castle Howard is slightly downhill, a nice start – the tea rooms tempt you straight away. If it's hot, a splendid avenue of trees on the way out of the village will offer some welcome shade.

2 Take the right fork, signed 'to Ganthorpe, York', 0.5 mile (800m) out of the village. Now you pay for your downhill as the road climbs to the top of **Cross Hill**, where there's a good view back to Terrington. The lane levels out as it passes through the stone cottages and farms of **Ganthorpe**. This hamlet was the birthplace of the historian, Arthur Toynbee (1886–1975) and the botanist, Richard Spruce (1817–93), who travelled to places like the Andes and the Amazon in search of specimens for scientific research. There's another short downhill section as the lane bends right by **Sata Wood**, then it's uphill again.

3 Turn left at the T-junction, where you get glimpses of a couple of the **Castle Howard domes**, then left at the crossroads following the directions to Slingsby and Castle Howard. The road, known as the **Stray**, is straight and madly undulating like a Roman road, with wide verges and avenues of trees lining the way. Some of the traffic is speedy so take care! Soon you pass beneath the extremely narrow stone arch of the Castle Howard estate's **Carrmire Gate**, which is flanked by castellated walls, then you come upon the gate house with its pyramidal roof. There's a roundabout next to a 100ft (91m) **obelisk** of 1714 dedicated

MAP: OS Explorer 300 Howardian Hills and Malton

START/FINISH: roadside parking in the main street, Terrington; grid ref: SE 670706

TRAILS/TRACKS: country lanes with some hills

LANDSCAPE: rolling pastoral hills and parkland

PUBLIC TOILETS: at Castle Howard

TOURIST INFORMATION: Malton, tel: 01653 600048

CYCLE HIRE: none locally

THE PUB: Bay Horse Inn, Terrington

🛈 The hilly terrain might be a little tiring for younger children. Take care on the Stray (Point 3) – some of the traffic here is faster than it should be

Getting to the start

From the A64 north east of York, follow the signs for Castle Howard and take the first left after the castle entrance. Alternatively, from Helmsley follow the B1257 signed 'Malton' to Slingsby and turn right for Castle Howard. Turn right by the castle's Great Lake.

Why do this cycle ride?

This pleasant ride combines the sophistication of the Castle Howard Estate and the simple beauty and rural charm of the Howardian Hills.

Researched and written by: John Gillham

to Lady Cecilia Howard. Here you need to decide whether or not to visit the palace (highly recommended).

4 Continuing down the Stray you'll pass the **Obelisk Ponds**, which are enshrouded by woodland, then the **Great Lake**, across which you get a great view of the palace and its many domes.

5 Turn left for 'Terrington' at the crossroads just beyond the lake. The lane soon swings right and climbs through the trees of **Shaw Wood**. If you have mountain bikes and

Neatly lawned houses at Terrington at the end of your ride

are experienced riders you could take the bridleway at the next bend (**South Bell Bottom**) then double back on the track over Husket and Ling Hills to meet the lane further west. If not, continue with the lane, which winds downhill across **Ganthorpe Moor** to meet the outward route by the first T-junction east of Terrington. Though you've still got the trees for shade, the downhill is now an uphill so you'll probably deserve that refreshment at the **Bay Horse Inn**.

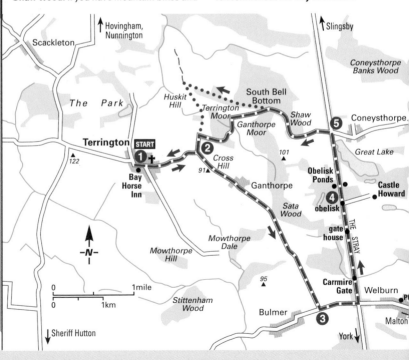

Bay Horse Inn

about the pub

Bay Horse Inn
Main Street, Terrington
Malton, North Yorkshire YO60 6PP
Tel: 01653 648416

DIRECTIONS: see Getting to the Start; pub in the village centre

PARKING: 30

OPEN: daily; all day

FOOD: daily; all day

BREWERY/COMPANY: free house

REAL ALE: Theakston Best, Black Sheep Riggwelter, John Smith's Cask, guest beers

ROOMS: 4 en suite

Terrington is an idyllic peaceful little village with stone cottages and greens, surrounded by the rolling Howardian Hills. The homely and friendly 400-year-old Bay Horse Inn, formerly a tailor's shop, reflects this rural charm from the outside to the interior. An archway of ivy surrounds the door of this whitewashed stone-built pub. Inside there's a welcoming log fire in the cosy lounge, while the public bar offers time-honoured pub games in the form of darts, dominoes, shove ha'penny and cribbage. At the back there's a conservatory adorned with old farm tools, and a small but attractively planted garden.

Food

Well-liked bar food takes in sandwiches, salads and sausage and mash and more substantial offerings like lambs' liver and onions, loin of pork in cider and apple cream sauce, steak and ale pie, and lamb shank with mash and fresh vegetables.

Family facilities

Families are very welcome inside the pub, especially in the conservatory. There's a typical children's menu and the garden is sheltered and safe for children.

Alternative refreshment stops

Tea Rooms, Terrington (by the post office); Hayloft and Lakeside Cafés at Castle Howard; The Malt Shovel, Hovingham – a fine pub just north of Terrington.

☛ Where to go from here

Don't miss out on exploring Castle Howard and its wonderful gardens and landscaped grounds (www.castlehoward.co.uk). Near Malton is the Eden Camp Modern History Theme Museum (www.edencamp.co.uk) which tells the story of civilian life in World War Two. Within reach is Nunnington Hall (www.nationaltrust.org.uk), Sherriff Hutton Castle and Yorkshire Lavender in Terrington.

Lastingham and Hutton-le-Hole

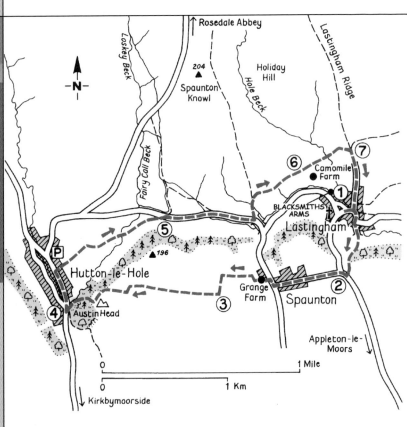

↑ Rosedale Abbey

Loskey Beck

Lastingham Ridge

–N–

204 ▲

Holiday Hill

Spaunton Knowl

Hole Beck

Fairy Call Beck

⑥   Camomile ● Farm   ⑦

①

BLACKSMITHS ARMS

Lastingham

Ⓟ

⑤

▲196

Hutton-le-Hole

③   Grange ● Farm

Spaunton

④ Austin Head

②

Appleton-le-Moors ↓

0 ———————— 1 Mile

0 ———————— 1 Km

↓ Kirkbymoorside

From St Cedd's monastery to the attractive village of Hutton-le-Hole.

Lastingham & Spaunton

St Cedd founded his monastery at Lastingham in 654. Nothing survives of his church but a Norman church was built in 1078 when the monastery was refounded after destruction in Danish raids in the 9th century.

Leaving Lastingham, the walk quickly reaches the only street in Spaunton. The village has hidden secrets; the fields here are set out on a Roman pattern, and at the beginning of the 19th century a Roman burial site was found near the village.

Pretty Hutton-le-Hole clusters around an irregular green and along the banks of the Hutton Beck. The village has an old Meeting House and a long association with the Society of Friends. Away from the village, near the end of the walk you'll come across a new local landmark. Marking the year 2000, the people of Lastingham placed a boulder carved with a cross on the hillside above the village. On it are two dates – AD 2000 and AD 654, the year in which St Cedd founded the original Lastingham monastery.

the walk

1 From the Blacksmiths Arms walk back down to the **green** and turn left, following signs to Cropton, Pickering and Rosedale. Where the road swings left, go right along a lane to wind over a small bridge and beside a **stream**. Ascend to a footpath sign, and go right, uphill, through a gate and through woodland to a handgate on to a road. Take the upper right fork lane, signed '**Spaunton**'.

2 Follow the road through Spaunton, and bend right at the end of the village, then turn left by the **public footpath sign** over the cattle grid into the **farmyard**. The waymarked track curves through the farm to reach another footpath sign, where the track bends left. At a large **outbuilding** the track bends left again.

3 After about 200yds (183m), follow a public footpath sign right and walk on to another sign as the track bends left. After 100yds (91m) take a footpath to the right, down the hill into **woodland**. Where the path divides, take the left fork down to a stile on your right, going off the track and down a steep grassy path into the valley. Descend

Pretty cottages line a quiet lane in Lastingham

2h00 – **4.5 MILES** – **7.2 KM** – **LEVEL 1**23

MAP: OS Explorer OL26 North York Moors – Western

START/FINISH: village street in Lastingham; grid ref: SE 729905

PATHS: farm tracks and field paths, 8 stiles

LANDSCAPE: moorland and woodland, with views

PUBLIC TOILETS: Hutton-le-Hole

TOURIST INFORMATION: Pickering, tel 01751 473791

THE PUB: The Blacksmiths Arms, Lastingham

Getting to the start

Lastingham is reached by turning north from the A170 Thirsk to Scarborough road between Kirkby Mills and Sinnington. Park sympathetically on the village street. Turn left by the church for the Blacksmith Arms.

Researched and written by:
John Gillham, David Winpenny

Lastingham NORTH YORKSHIRE

beside a stream to a stile by a gate, which takes you on to the road in **Hutton-le-Hole**.

4 Turn right up the main street. After passing the **Barn Hotel** and the Wychwood Gifts shop turn right, following a route signed to Lastingham. Beyond a gate, pass through a garden and to the right of some **sheds** to reach a stile, which gives entry to a large field that is sometimes used as a campsite. Turn left and follow the edge of the field and over two more stiles to a kissing gate before a **footbridge**. Follow the path through woodland to a gate and follow the grassy track to the road.

5 Turn right and follow the road for 0.5 mile (800m) and turn left at a footpath sign just before the road descends to a stone bridge. A rutted track bends right between farmland on the right and **Spaunton Moor**.

6 Just before **Camomile Farm**, leave the track on the left and follow the footpath sign and waymarker posts to round a **copse** of sycamores, beyond which you descend

into a valley. Cross over the stream to a stile and a kissing gate. Continue walking with the wall on your right-hand side to another kissing gate and stile, which will lead you to a **carved stone** with a cross and a three-pointed sign.

7 Turn right, downhill, through a gate and on to the metalled road that descends to the village of **Lastingham**.

what to look for

There is a full range of activities at the Ryedale Folk Museum in Hutton-le-Hole (www.ryedalefolkmuseum.co.uk), where old structures from around the North York Moors have been reconstructed as a hamlet. As well as an authentic Elizabethan manor house with a massive oak cruck frame, farm buildings, cottages and traditional long houses, you can see an early photographer's studio, a medieval glass kiln and a variety of agricultural tools and transport. There's also a fire engine and a hearse. Maypole dancing, rare breeds days and quilting are just some of the activities that take place during the year and you may catch the historic farm machinery working, or have the chance to try your hand at some of the almost-forgotten crafts.

Visitors examining the shop fronts in the Ryedale Folk Museum, Hutton-le-Hole

The Blacksmiths Arms

A charming stone-built inn dating from 1693 and unspoilt by progress, situated in a beautiful village that is part of a conservation area. Antiquity is evident everywhere, from the pretty York-stone building to the flagged and beamed bar, and the range that houses the open log fire is 200 years old. Even the furnishings are in keeping with the pub's great age. There are excellent changing real ales from micro-breweries and a wide-ranging pub food menu, as well as three cosy, cottagey bedrooms.

Food
Bar snacks include sandwiches, filled Yorkshire puddings and home-made soups, while the main menu and specials board offer beer-battered cod, steak and ale pie, lamb and mint pie, crispy roast duck with orange sauce, Yorkshire hotpot and a roast of the day. Good vegetarian options. Afternoon teas.

Family facilities
Children are welcome inside the pub. No children's menu but smaller portions are available, as are high chairs.

Alternative refreshment stops
There is a range of cafés, tea rooms, restaurants and pubs in Hutton-le-Hole – the Barn Hotel Tea Rooms and the Crown Hotel are recommended. In Lastingham, the excellent Lastingham Grange offers dinner and light lunches, as well as a full Sunday lunch, but is closed from mid-November to March.

☞ Where to go from here
If you're a real ale enthusiast, the Cropton Brewery and Visitor Centre (www.croptonbrewery.co.uk), 1.5 miles (2.4km) east of Lastingham, is the place to head for. Visit the Beck Isle Museum of Rural Life in Pickering (www.beckislemuseum.co.uk) or visit the Ryedale Folk Museum in Hutton-le-Hole.

about the pub

The Blacksmiths Arms
Front Street, Lastingham
North Yorkshire YO62 6TL
Tel: 01751 417247

DIRECTIONS: see Getting to the Start
PARKING: roadside parking
OPEN: daily; all day May to October; closed Tuesday lunchtime November to April
FOOD: daily; all day May to October
BREWERY/COMPANY: free house
REAL ALE: Lastingham Ale, two micro-brewery guest beers
DOGS: in garden only
ROOMS: 3 en suite

Kirkham Priory and the Derwent Valley

CYCLE

A circular ride around the peaceful Derwent Valley.

Kirkham Priory

Sometime in the early 1120s, William L'Espec was riding by the banks of the Derwent when his horse threw him. He died instantly. Grief-stricken, his father, Lord Helmsley, founded an Augustinian monastery on the site of the accident.

The priory started as a small church in 1125, but by the middle of the 13th century fine western towers had been built and the eastern end extended. Later chapels were added, one abutting the north transept, and a second by the presbytery's south wall. The money ran out and the work was halted. Unfortunately, Kirkham's lack of size didn't save it from destruction during the Dissolution of the Monasteries, when it was laid to waste.

The main tower of the priory collapsed in 1784 during high winds, and locals took much of the masonry to build their own houses. However the remains that survive do much to stir the imagination. Today, it's a rather peaceful setting with lawns sloping

The remains of Kirkham Priory

down to the river and sylvan hillsides beyond. The wall of the 13th-century gatehouse is the centrepiece, with fine sculpted figures representing, among others, Christ, St George and the Dragon, St Bartholomew and David and Goliath. Also of note are the delicate arches of the lavatorium, set in the west wall of the cloister.

the ride

1 Westow is a pleasant little hillside village lying half a mile (800m) above the River Derwent. Strangely the name originates from Wifestowe, meaning a place of women. The pub, the Blacksmith's Inn, is the centrepiece of the village as the church lies in isolation a mile to the north. Head north from the village centre then go left at the first junction, signed Kirkham and York. Although there's a bridleway on the right, it's usually too choked with vegetation to be of any use. It would be better to stay with the lane, passing the solitary electricity-generating **windmill** to arrive at a T-junction at the northern extremities of Howsham Wood. Turn right here, tracing the brow of **Badger Bank** high above the River Derwent. After staying fairly level along the bank, the lane makes a steady descent to the **Stone Trough Inn** at Kirkham.

2 From the inn the road descends steadily downhill, around a left-hand bend and past a small **car park** by the entrance to the priory, which is well worth a visit before you continue the journey. The road continues over **Kirkham Bridge**, an elegant three-arched stone structure, rebuilt in the 18th century.

2h00 — **8 MILES** — **12.9 KM** — **LEVEL 1 2 3**

MAP: OS Explorer 300 Howardian Hills and Malton

START/FINISH: roadside parking in Westow; grid ref: SE 753653

TRAILS/TRACKS: all quiet country lanes

LANDSCAPE: rolling pastoral hills and a wooded valley

PUBLIC TOILETS: none on route

TOURIST INFORMATION: Malton, tel: 01653 600048

CYCLE HIRE: none locally

THE PUB: The Stone Trough Inn, Kirkham Abbey

❶ Some of the hills are fairly steep and challenging and would be tiring for young children

Getting to the start

Westow lies just off the A64 York to Malton road. Leave the A64 near Whitwell-on-the-Hill, following signs for Kirkham. Descend into the Derwent Valley past the priory. Go straight on at the junction to pass The Stone Trough Inn, turn left at the next junction, then right to reach the village centre. Park at the roadside.

Why do this cycle ride?

Here you can see the Derwent Valley at its most attractive, with great loops in the lively river, wooded hillsides, great mansions and a fascinating ancient priory.

Researched and written by: John Gillham

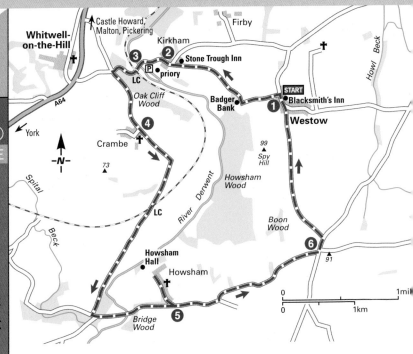

3 At the other side there's a level crossing followed by a short steep pull (you may need to dismount), as the road climbs through the dense conifers of **Oak Cliff Wood** to two closely spaced junctions. Ignore the right turns at both but instead follow signs to Crambe. The lane now follows the upper perimeter of the conifer wood before descending towards **Crambe** village.

4 This quiet backwater lies on a cul-de-sac to the right, so there's a there-and-back detour to this same spot to see the square-towered **St Michael's Church**. It's downhill from here, with a right-hand bend after 0.5 mile (800m). Beyond this you come to another **level crossing**. This one has a bell to ring to get the attention of the signalman, who will come to open it for you – it's all good 21st-century technology here in the Howardian Hills! The road descends further with the River Derwent clearly in view below left and the grand mansion of **Howsham Hall**

on the far bank. At the next T-junction turn left following the directions to 'Howsham and Leavening', but ignore the right turn shortly after. Your road crosses the Derwent at Howsham Bridge, before climbing steadily past **Bridge Wood**.

5 Howsham village lies on another cul-de-sac to the left. Its cottages have well-manicured greens; there's a small spired **church** on the right and the well-known and rather grand **Howsham Hall School** at the end of the road. Back on the main route, the lane climbs and winds over pastured knolls and after 3 miles (4.8km) comes to a high crossroads.

6 Turn left for Westow and Malton, then take the left fork for **Westow**. The road makes a gentle ascent to a rise east of **Spy Hill**. Now you descend back to Westow village.

The Stone Trough Inn

about the pub

The Stone Trough Inn
Kirkham Abbey,
Whitwell-on-the-Hill,
York, North Yorkshire YO60 7JS
Tel 01653 618713
www.stonetroughinn.co.uk

DIRECTIONS: see Getting to the start	
PARKING: 100	
OPEN: all day Sunday; closed Monday except Bank Holidays	
FOOD: no food Sunday evening	
BREWERY/COMPANY: free house	
REAL ALE: Tetley, Black Sheep, Timothy Taylor Landlord, Malton Golden Chance, Theakston Old Peculier, guest beer	

Restored in 1982 from the original Stone Trough Cottage, the Stone Trough Inn stands beside a narrow lane high above Kirkham Abbey and the River Derwent. Lots of oak beams, bare stone walls, flagged floors and cosy rooms filled with fresh flowers add colour and character, and log fires and comfortable furnishings draw a good crowd. Further attractions include the super views across the Derwent Valley and the impressive, modern pub menus that make the most of the abundant local produce available. Good global list of wines and four tip-top Yorkshire ales on tap.

Food
In the bar you'll find excellent lunchtime sandwiches (cheddar cheese and red onion), starters of warm salad of crispy chilli beef with honey and sesame seed dressing and home-made soup, and main courses such as local pork sausages on sage and onion rosti with real ale gravy, creamy fish pie, roast monkfish wrapped in Parma ham with rosemary butter sauce, and whole roast partridge with crab-apple jus. Puddings include treacle tart with vanilla ice cream. Separate restaurant menu.

Family facilities
Children of all ages are welcome. You'll find a children's menu and portions of adult dishes, high chairs, small cutlery and drawing materials to keep youngsters amused.

Alternative refreshment stops
The Blacksmith's Arms, Westow.

☞ Where to go from here
The Cistercian Rievaulx Abbey, a short way to the north, has connections with Kirkham, and is well worth seeing (www.english-heritage.org.uk). Castle Howard (www.castlehoward.co.uk) is a short drive away, as is Pickering and the North Yorkshire Moors Railway, a fascinating steam railway that travels through stunning scenery into the heart of the moor (www.northyorkshiremoorsrailway.com).

Moorland around Goathland and Mallyan Spout

From the popular moorland village with its television links, through woodland and over the moor.

Heartbeat country

Goathland is one of the most popular destinations for visitors to the North York Moors National Park. Its situation, around a large open common, criss-crossed by tracks and closely cropped by grazing sheep, has always been attractive. Today many tourists are drawn to Goathland because it is used as the fictitious village of Aidensfield for the popular television series *Heartbeat*. The Goathland Story exhibition tells the village's history from the time it was an Iron Age centre for making stone querns to grind corn, to today – and there's a special *Heartbeat* collection. The walk begins with a visit to the 70ft (21m) Mallyan Spout

waterfall into the West Beck. In dry weather only a trickle of water may fall from the side of the gorge into the stream below but after rain it can become an impressive torrent. Take care at all times: sometimes it may be impossible to pass the waterfall on the streamside path.

After you have crossed the ford and turned on to the moorland by Hunt House, you might find yourself accompanied by the sudden flutter of red grouse rising from their nest sites on the heather moorland.

If you visit in late summer, the moors will be clothed in the colours of heather. Sheep grazing has for centuries been the traditional way of managing the moors as the animals help keep the heather short and encourage the new shoots. To regenerate the heather, landowners regularly use carefully controlled burning in the early spring or the autumn when the ground is wet. The fire burns away the old heather stems, but does not damage the roots, nor the peat. New growth quickly springs up to feed the young grouse.

what to look for

In the valley of the West Beck, and especially near Mallyan Spout, you will see lots of ferns. Among the sorts you might spot are the male fern, with its pale green stems, the buckler fern, which has scales with a dark central stripe and paler edges, and the hartstongue fern, with its distinctive strap-like fronds. They are all typical of damp, humid areas, and like every fern, they are flowerless. Instead, they reproduce by means of spores – look under the leaves to find the characteristic dots that are the spore sacs or sporangia. The spores are dispersed by wind or by animals.

Water splashing down rocks at Mallyan Spout

WALK

2h00 — **4.5 MILES** — **7.2 KM** — **LEVEL 1 2 3**

MAP: OS Explorer OL27 North York Moors – Eastern

START/FINISH: west end of Goathland village, near church; grid ref: NZ 827007

PATHS: streamside tracks, field and moorland paths, 2 stiles

LANDSCAPE: deep, wooded valley, farmland and open moorland

PUBLIC TOILETS: Goathland village

TOURIST INFORMATION: Whitby, tel 01947 602674

THE PUB: The Goathland Hotel, Goathland

❶ The initial riverside path to Mallyan Spout is slippery

Getting to the start

Goathland is situated 8 miles (12.9km) southwest of Whitby. It lies just 2 miles (3.2km) west of the A169 Whitby to Malton road and can also be reached using the North Yorkshire Moors Railway from Grosmont or Pickering. The easiest parking is at the west end of the village near the church.

Researched and written by:
John Gillham, David Winpenny

Goathland

NORTH YORKSHIRE

the walk

1 Opposite the church go through the kissing gate to the right of the **Mallyan Spout Hotel**, signed 'Mallyan Spout'. Follow the path to a streamside signpost and turn left. Continue past the waterfall (take care after heavy rain). Follow the footpath signs, over two footbridges, over a stile and up steps. Continue by the stream, then ascend to a stile on to a road beside a **bridge**.

2 Turn left along the road and climb the hill. Where the road bends left, go right along a **bridleway** through a gate. Turn left down a path to go over a bridge, then ahead by the **buildings**, through a gate and across the field.

3 Part-way across the field, go through a gate to the right into **woodland**. Ascend a stony track, go through a wooden

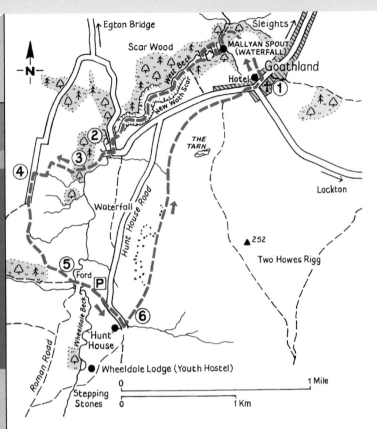

↑ Egton Bridge   Sleights ↗

Scar Wood   MALLYAN SPOUT (WATERFALL)

Goathland

Hotel

① Lockton

THE TARN

Waterfall

Hunt House Road

West Beck   New Wath Scar

② ③ ④

▲ 252

Two Howes Rigg

⑤ Ford

P

Wheeldale Beck

Hunt House

⑥

Roman Road

● Wheeldale Lodge (Youth Hostel)

Stepping Stones

0   1 Mile

0   1 Km

gate then left to another gate on the edge of the wood. Ignoring the gate, turn right up the field, before going left at the top through a **gateway**. Continue with a wall on your right and go through a waymarked gateway in the wall and up the field, to emerge through a gate on to a **metalled lane**.

4 Turn left along the lane, go through a gate and follow the **'Roman Road'** sign. Go through another gate, still following the public bridleway signs as you join a green lane. Continue through a small handgate, to descend to another gate and then on until you reach a **ford**.

5 Cross the ford and go straight ahead along the track, eventually to reach a road by a **bungalow**. Turn right up the road and left by a **wooden garage** to continue along a green track up the hillside.

6 Go straight ahead at a crossing track, passing a small **cairn** and bending left along the heathery ridge. The obvious path is marked by a series of **little cairns**. Eventually, take a left fork to go down a shallow gill and join a clear track. **Goathland church** soon comes into sight. Pass a bridleway sign and descend to the road near the church. The **Goathland Hotel** can be found on the right-hand side at the far end of the main street.

The Goathland Hotel

Conveniently sited on Goathland's main street, just 500 yards (457m) from the North Yorkshire Moors Railway, this stone-built Victorian building draws the crowds despite its off-the-beaten-track moorland village location. It is the Aidensfield Arms in the TV series Heartbeat *and can get very busy with 'location' enthusiasts, so arrive early! Traditionally furnished, it has a spacious main bar with tiled floor, ceiling beams and winter log fires, a plush, carpeted lounge bar, and a wood-panelled restaurant. Comfortable bedrooms have moorland views.*

Food

Food is simple but well prepared. At lunchtime expect open sandwiches (home-cooked ham) and salads, ploughman's lunches and traditional bar meals like filled giant Yorkshire puddings (roast beef and onion gravy), home-made steak and kidney pie, and Whitby scampi and chips.

Family facilities

There are two family areas in the bars and smaller portions of adult dishes are available. Good-sized rear garden and three bedrooms with extra beds or cots for families.

Alternative refreshment stops

As you would expect from a popular village, there are cafés and snack bars dotted around Goathland, as well as ice-cream vans on the green. The

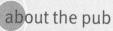

about the pub

The Goathland Hotel
Goathland, Whitby
North Yorkshire YO22 5LY
Tel: 01947 896203

DIRECTIONS: on main village street	
PARKING: 20	
OPEN: daily; all day in high summer	
FOOD: daily	
BREWERY/COMPANY: Punch Taverns	
REAL ALE: Flowers IPA, Camerons Strongarm	
DOGS: welcome on leads	
ROOMS: 9 bedrooms (8 en suite)	

restaurant at the Mallyan Spout Hotel has a fine reputation.

☛ Where to go from here

Take a nostalgic trip on the North Yorkshire Moors Railway, which has a station in the valley below the village. It runs through Newtondale between Pickering and Grosmont and ran steam trains from 1847 until it was closed in 1957. It reopened in 1973 and most of its trains are steam-hauled (www.northyorkshiremoors railway .com).

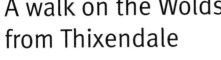

A walk on the Wolds from Thixendale

From the hidden village of Thixendale over chalk hills and through dry valleys.

Going the Wolds Way

Chalk underlies the Yorkshire Wolds. Unlike the harder rocks of the dales and the moors, the Wolds chalk is soft and permeable, so the landscape around here is one of rounded hills and deep dry valleys. Our walk is through rich farming land – indeed, these slopes have been cultivated since Neolithic people set up home here more than 5,000 years ago.

More than half the walk follows the Wolds Way, a 79 mile (127km) National Trail that runs from the bridge over the Humber Estuary to Filey Brigg. Much of the walk follows the Centenary Way, established by North Yorkshire County Council in 1989 to mark 100 years of local government.

Some say that Thixendale is named from the six dry valleys that meet here. The more imaginative reckon to count 16 converging dales. Place-name dictionaries, more prosaically, derive it from a Viking called Sigstein. Whatever its origin, Thixendale is one of the most remote of the Wolds villages, approached by deep, winding dry valleys between steep chalk escarpments. It has a number of old cottages, but much of its character is due to local landowner Sir Tatton Sykes in the later part of the 19th century. As well as building estate cottages, he contributed the church, the school and the former vicarage. Do visit the church – the stained glass by Clayton and Bell, showing the Days of Creation, is great fun, especially the flamingos and the fearsome waterspout.

Sir Tatton Sykes was a great church-builder and philanthropist – and an even greater eccentric. He insisted that his body needed to maintain an even temperature, and was known to stick his bare feet out of the windows of railway carriages to make sure. As he warmed up on his walks he would shed clothing, paying local boys to return it to the house. He even wore two pairs of trousers to preserve decency as he divested himself. Flowers were a great hate; he had the estate gardens ploughed up and told his tenants that the only kind of flowers they could grow were cauliflowers.

the walk

1 Leave the Cross Keys and turn right down Thixendale's village street, passing the church and the Old Post Office. Just beyond the last house on the right, go up a track, following the **Wolds Way/Centenary Way** sign. Cross over a ladder stile in a wire fence on your right and continue walking up the track as it curves right around the hillside.

2 As you approach the top of the hill, watch out on the left for a **Wolds Way sign**, which takes you left along a grassy track. Go over a ladder stile then along the field side to join the track again.

3 At the next **Wolds Way sign** leave the track to go over a stile where you continue with the **wire fence** on your left. At the top of the field go right by the sign. The path descends to reach a stile and descends steeply into a dry valley. Halfway along the descent, go over a stile, partially hidden by bushes to the left. Descend further to another **waymarked stile**, then to a stile by a gate at the bottom.

4 Follow the blue **public bridleway sign** to the right, winding left up the side

| 2h00 | 4 MILES | 6.4 KM | LEVEL 1 2 3 |

MAP: OS Explorer 300 Howardian Hills & Malton
START/FINISH: Thixendale village street near the church; grid ref: SE 842611
PATHS: clear tracks and field paths, 9 stiles
LANDSCAPE: deep, dry valleys and undulating farm land
PUBLIC TOILETS: none on route
TOURIST INFORMATION: Malton, tel 01653 600048
THE PUB: Cross Keys, Thixendale
! Under 14s not allowed inside pub

Getting to the start

Thixendale lies secluded in a little valley 3 miles (4.8km) north of the A166 York to Bridlington road, 9 miles (14.5km) south of Malton. From the south, leave the A166 at Fridaythorpe and take the left fork at the end of the village, or from the north, take the B1248, then the second left at Wharram le Street. Park in the village street near the Cross Keys.

Researched and written by:
John Gillham, David Winpenny

valley. Near the top of the valley is a deep **earthwork ditch**; cross over a stile and continue along the edge of the field. Where the footpath divides go right through the patch of **woodland** on to a track by a signpost.

5 Turn right and follow the **Wolds Way sign**. Follow this clear field-edge path for 0.75 mile (1.2km). At the end of the woodland on your right, look out for a signpost. Turn right here, now following the **Centenary Way**, going down the edge of the field and passing a ruined building with a **tall chimney**. Follow the winding footpath past a signpost.

6 At the next signpost turn right off the track, signed '**Centenary Way**'. Walk down the field side on a grassy track. At the field end leave the track and go through a **waymarked gate**. The path goes left and passes along the hillside to descend to a stile beside a gate.

7 Follow the **yellow waymark** straight ahead across the field (pathless on ground), then pass to the left of a row of trees. A path develops and descends to the right of the village **cricket field** to reach a lane by some houses. This leads back to the **Cross Keys** and out onto the village street.

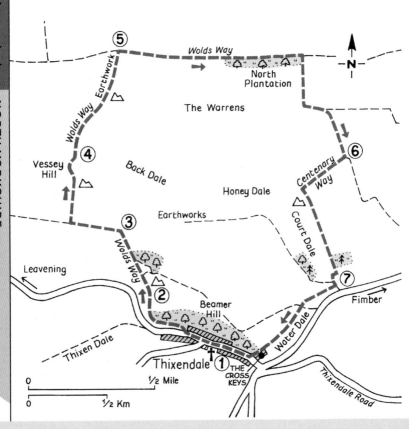

Cross Keys

Although this former 18th-century farmhouse has an unassuming appearance – plain whitewashed exterior with green and blue paintwork – it is one of the hidden gems in the Wolds. Simple, unspoilt and a very traditional village local, popular with walkers and cyclists, you'll find a single, welcoming and very cosy L-shaped bar with fitted wall benches, a relaxing atmosphere, well-kept beer and good value home-cooked food. Blissfully free of intrusive piped music and gaming machines, but there is a juke box that only plays old songs. Bedrooms are housed within a converted stable and provide a peaceful base from which to explore the surrounding rolling countryside.

Food

The short menu offers home-made soups, ploughman's lunches, roast beef sandwiches, steak buns, home-made pasties, sausage, egg and chips, and local game dishes in season. Good nursery puddings like treacle tart, sticky toffee pudding and toffee apple crumble.

Family facilities

Facilities are limited as children under 14 years are not allowed inside the pub. However, there is a super, sun-trap rear garden for fine weather eating and drinking.

Alternative refreshment stops

Behind Thixendale Store and Post Office is a café (closed Fridays), offering breakfast, lunch, teas and snacks.

☞ Where to go from here

Visit Sir Tatton Syke's home, Sledmere House. An elegant Georgian mansion, largely designed by Sir Christopher Sykes in 1751, it has superb plasterwork, an elegant staircase and attractive grounds. At the Eden Camp Modern History Theme Museum (www.edencamp.co.uk) near Malton, relive the civilian way of life during World War II through the sights, sounds and smells of those dangerous years. Castle Howard of Brideshead Revisited fame is just a short drive away (www.castlehoward.co.uk).

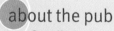

about the pub

Cross Keys

Thixendale, Malton
North Yorkshire YO17 9TG
Tel: 01377 288272

DIRECTIONS:	see Getting to the start
PARKING:	village street
OPEN:	daily
FOOD:	daily
BREWERY/COMPANY:	free house
REAL ALE:	Tetley, Jennings Bitter, guest beer
DOGS:	in garden only
ROOMS:	3 en suite

Thixendale NORTH YORKSHIRE

Dalby Forest

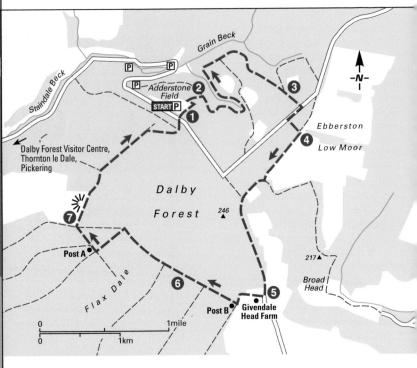

A short ride through the forest where you seek the wildlife that's watching you.

The Forest

In 1919, when the Forestry Commission was founded, Britain's woodland cover had shrunk to around 5 per cent, which meant we had to import large quantities of timber to meet the increasing needs of industry. In Yorkshire they turned to Dalby on the south east corner of the North York Moors. The area, once part of the Royal Hunting Forest of Pickering, had degenerated into boggy heathland, poverty-stricken

upland farms and a huge rabbit warren that provided fur for a felt hat industry. Several streams drained the moorland plateau and flowed south west into Dalby Beck, forming a rigg and dale landscape. Scrub oak and birch clustered around these streams, but in general the ground was only suitable for conifers. By 1921 the planting began and within years over 8,500 acres (3,442ha) of Sitka Spruce and Scots Pine had covered the ground.

Conservationists hated these new forests, complaining that wildlife had been decimated, but today, if you stay quiet and look hard enough, you'll see that it's really quite abundant. In quieter corners you may

CYCLE

2h00 · **6 MILES** · **9.7 KM** · **LEVEL 1 2 3**

stumble upon the Bambi-like roe deer. Many of the mammals, such as the pygmy shrew and the otter, stay clear of humans and it's bird-life you're more likely to spot. Besides the common blue tits, you're quite likely to see a wading heron, or a tiny warbler such as that summer visitor, the chiffchaf, so called because of its birdsong.

the ride

1 The **green cycle route** begins beyond the trees at the south east end of the large **Adderstone Field** (the furthest from the visitor centre). Here you turn left along a narrow slightly downhill track. Though still easy, it's the most difficult section of the route – use gentle braking if you're a little unsure. Ignore two lesser, unsigned left fork tracks.

2 Turn right along a much wider forestry track which takes a winding course round the afforested valley of **Worry Gill**. Where the more demanding red route goes off on a rough track to the right, your green route goes straight on, still using a well-graded track.

3 Where a track doubles back, go straight on up a steady hill before meeting the **forest drive** again. Cross this with care – it can be quite busy on summer weekends – before turning right along it for 200yds (183m). Turn left along a narrow path signed with red and green waymarkers and just before a 30 mile per hour speed limit sign (hope you were not speeding!). If you're early and it's summer, you may be able to dally and eat some of the bilberries that grow beside the path.

MAP: OS Explorer OL27 North York Moors Eastern Area

START/FINISH: car park at Adderstone Field, Dalby Forest; grid ref: SE 883897

TRAILS/TRACKS: forestry roads and a few narrow paths, mostly well graded

LANDSCAPE: conifer forest

PUBLIC TOILETS: Visitor Centre, Lower Dalby (not on route)

TOURIST INFORMATION: Dalby Forest Visitor Centre, tel 01751 460295

CYCLE HIRE: Cycle Hire Kiosk next to Visitor Centre, Low Dalby, tel 01751 460400

THE PUB: New Inn, Thornton le Dale, off the route

⚠ There's a short, rough and slightly downhill section of track at the start. The forest drive road needs to be crossed with care twice

Getting to the start

From the A170 at Thornton le Dale head north on a minor road signed the Dalby Forest, then turn off right on the Dalby Forest Drive, where you'll come to the tollbooths. Adderstone Field, the start of the ride, lies about 5 miles (8km) beyond the visitor centre.

Why do this cycle ride?

It's a good introduction to forest tracks, with just a few hilly bits to get your pulse racing, but nothing frightening to put off the inexperienced. There's lots of wildlife for the observant cyclist.

Researched and written by: John Gillham

4 The path reaches a **flinted road** at the south east edge of the forest. Turn right along this then left at the next junction. Looking left, you'll see the rougher high pastures of **Ebberston Low Moor** decline to the greener, more fertile fields of the **Vale of Pickering**.

5 Turn right just before reaching **Givendale Head Farm** along a rutted farm track with a grassy island in the middle. Turn right at the next junction (**Post B**) on a downhill section, followed by an uphill one where you're joined by a **farm track** from the left.

6 A long hill follows to a wide junction where you go straight on along a tarred lane. A sign tells you that you're now at the head of **Flaxdale**. Stay with the tarred lane at the next bend and junction. Turn right at the crossroads along a long sandy track (**Post A**), then right again at the next junction. Note the **linear earthwork** to both left and right – nobody seems to know the exact origins of these.

7 After going straight on at the next junction past a fine stand of **Scots pines**, you get fine views over the farm pastures of High Rigg to **Levisham Moor**. There's another downhill section followed by an uphill one. Take a right fork at **Newclose Rigg**. Where the red route goes straight on, your green route veers right along the main track. There's a downhill left curve beyond which you take the **upper right fork**, which brings the route back to the forest drive opposite Adderstone Field.

Top: A track in Dalby Forest

New Inn

A Georgian coaching inn in the centre of a picturesque village complete with beck running beside the main street, and village stocks and market cross. The inn retains its old-world charm, with log fires, low beamed ceiling, traditional furniture and hand-pulled ales.

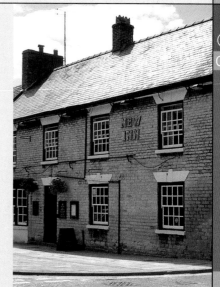

Food

Freshly cooked food is one of the pub's attractions, with many tempting choices on the interesting menu and specials board: medallions of beef fillet, pan-fried chicken supreme, grilled halibut steak, rack of lamb, and salmon fillet with baby cucumber show the range of main courses.

Family facilities

Children are welcome in the dining area if eating and they have their own menu.

Alternative refreshment stops

There's a café and kiosk at the Dalby Forest Visitor Centre.

☛ Where to go from here

The Beck Isle Museum at Pickering houses many photos and artefacts that will show you the local customs. The museum follows the historical developments in social and domestic life of the last two centuries (www.beckislemuseum.co.uk). Re-live the golden age of steam with a ride on the North Yorkshire Moors Railway, Britain's most popular heritage railway, through 18 miles (29km)of stunning scenery (www.northyorkshiremoorsrailway.com).

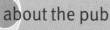

about the pub

New Inn

Maltongate, Thornton le Dale
Pickering, North Yorkshire YO18 7LF
Tel: 01751 474226

DIRECTIONS: beside the A170 in the centre of the village
PARKING: 15
OPEN: daily; all day in summer
FOOD: daily
BREWERY/COMPANY: Scottish & Newcastle
REAL ALE: Theakston Black Bull, John Smith's, Greene King Old Speckled Hen
ROOMS: 6 en suite

Warter Wold

Warter Wold

EAST YORKSHIRE

A pleasant countryside ride discovering the rolling Yorkshire Wolds and some charming villages.

uninhabitable swamps. These settlers made clearings and left much evidence of their existence in the form of burial mounds (tumuli) and earthwork dykes – you'll see one of those from the bridleway south of Huggate.

The Yorkshire Wolds

The Yorkshire Wolds form the most northerly outcrop of chalk in Britain. Here, smooth, rounded hills top shallow valleys with streams trickling through grass and woodlands. Chalk makes rich fertile ground for farming and the prehistoric settlers did just that. In those days the hills were tree-covered, good for providing cover from wild animals, while the valleys were

The Romans conquered the region but settled quite peaceably here; you'll be riding along one of their roads into Warter. But the Normans were a little more brutal – William the Conqueror, angered by the resistance of the locals, set about his 'harrying of the North'. The whole area was sacked and set ablaze. Gone were the trees. The Wolds people never replanted them – some say it is because they believed that witches could hide behind them.

The Enclosure Acts of the late 1700s brought more significant changes. The large, straight-edged fields with long hawthorn hedges were set up then, allowing the patchwork of pasture and cornfields you see today. Villages like Warter and North Dalton had popped up in the valleys to be near the water table – look out for the dewponds and the water pumps.

the ride

1 From the car park, cycle back to the village green and turn right past the old **church**. Take the first right, a narrow road climbing steeply at first with a shallow grassy vale to the left.

2 There's a T-junction at the top of the hill, where you turn left signed '**Market Weighton & Dalton'**, on the level, at first, then, beyond a left-hand bend, an easy descent. By a red-bricked house and a narrow wood turn right, highlighted by a **Middleton signpost**. After the first bend the road passes some high manicured hedges then beneath magnificent beech trees near **Middleton Lodge**.

3 The lane comes to a junction on the northern edge of **Middleton-on-the-Wolds**. Turn right if you want to have a look around then return to the same spot, or left past a **post box** and the last houses to continue the journey. From the top of the first hill there are fine views northwards across the rolling Wolds. There's a small

Looking across Warter Wold from the Bridleway

5h00 – **15 MILES** – **24 KM** – **LEVEL 123**

MAP: OS Explorer 294 Market Weighton & Yorkshire Wolds Central

START/FINISH: Warter village car park; grid ref: SE868502

TRAILS/TRACKS: country lanes, some hilly and an easy section of grass-track bridleway

LANDSCAPE: rolling hills

PUBLIC TOILETS: none on route

TOURIST INFORMATION: York, tel 01904 621756

CYCLE HIRE: none locally

THE PUB: Wolds Inn, Huggate

🚫 A long route with some hills. Not suitable for young children

Getting to the start
Leave the York ring road on the A1079, then at Barmby Moor take the Pocklington turn-off (B1246) to the left. Warter lies 5 miles (8km) along this road. Turn right at the village green to the signed village car park.

Why do this cycle ride?
If you want a good summer's day ride and would like to sample the Yorkshire Wolds without taking to mountain biking, this is your route.

Researched and written by: John Gillham

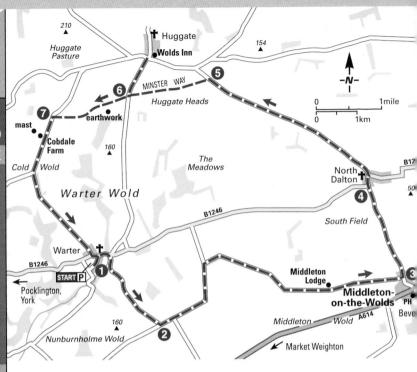

dip preceding a steady climb into Dalton village, where you meet the B road at the apex of a bend.

4 Go straight on towards the village centre where there's a splendid duck pond, then go left by the **Methodist chapel**. The road climbs steadily and is pleasant with flower-decked verges.

5 After 3 miles (4.8km) turn left by a large **ash tree** on to a wide, rutted, grassy bridleway, part of the Minster Way. This firm track, lined by thorn bushes to the right and thistles to the left, eases across **Huggate Heads**. To the south the fields fall away into a shallow wooded vale. After 1.5 miles (2.4km) the bridleway comes to another lane.

6 Turn right to reach **Huggate**, and the **Wolds Inn**. Return along the lane to the bridleway. This time turn right on a similar

grass track, which winds around hillsides above two steep-sided grassy vales so typical of the Yorkshire Wolds.

7 Just beyond the second the track comes to the road. Climb left, past the communications mast and **Cobdale Farm**, then take the left fork, signed 'Warter'. It's the course of a Roman road, which, beyond **Lings Plantation**, makes a long steady descent. Brake gently here to control your speed. At the bottom of the hill lies **Warter** and an old building with a clock, dated 1868. Turn left here, then right at the green to pass a charming terrace of **whitewashed cottages** with thatched roofs and porches fronted by the quaint cast-iron street lamps from the Victorian era. The road leads back to the car park.

Wolds Inn

about the pub

Wolds Inn
Driffield Road, Huggate
Pocklington, East Yorkshire YO42 1YH
Tel: 01377 288217

DIRECTIONS: village signposted south off
A166 between York and Driffield. Pub in
village centre
PARKING: 45
OPEN: closed all day Monday and Friday
lunch (except Bank Holidays)
FOOD: daily
BREWERY/COMPANY: free house
REAL ALE: Tetley, Timothy Taylor Landlord,
summer guest beer
ROOMS: 3 en suite

*Probably the highest inn on the Yorkshire
Wolds, this venerable village local, close
to the parish church, also claims 16th-
century origins. Beneath a huddle of
tiled roofs and white-painted chimneys,
it sports an interior of wood
panelling, gleaming
brassware and open fires.
Separate locals' games
room and good real ale on
tap. Pleasant rear garden
with views of the
surrounding Wolds. A great
favourite with cyclists.*

Food
Baguettes and sandwiches
line up alongside bar main
dishes of gammon and egg,
home-made steak pie,
grilled fillet of plaice, pork chops and
mushrooms, and a weekly changing curry.
A typical restaurant meal may feature cod
and pancetta fishcakes, followed by rack of
lamb cooked in garlic, or decent steaks with
all the trimmings. Sunday roast lunches.

Family facilities
Children are very welcome inside the pub.
There's a children's menu, smaller portions
of adult dishes are also available, notably
good-value Sunday lunches, and there are
high chairs.

Alternative refreshment stops
The Star Inn at North Dalton.

☛ Where to go from here
Head off to see Burnby Hall Gardens and
Stuart Collection in Pocklington, where
there are 9 acres (3.6ha) of beautiful
gardens with lakes, woodland walks and
a Victorian garden to explore. In Beverley,
the Museum of Army Transport tells the
story of army transport from horse-drawn
wagons to the present.

Wheels through the Wolds

CYCLE

The Wolds

EAST YORKSHIRE

Gentle riding through rich, rolling farmland.

The Hudson Way

The route takes its name from George Hudson (1800–71), originally from Howsham, about 20 miles (32km) away, who became known as the 'Railway King'. Hudson was a financier (and sometimes a less than scrupulous one) rather than an engineer, who masterminded many of the great railway projects in the boom years of the middle 19th century. The line from York,

Cycling out of South Dalton

via Market Weighton to Beverley, was a relatively small part of his empire.

There are abundant opportunities for wildlife-spotting all along the railway route, but Kiplingcotes Chalk Pit is of particular interest. First worked in the 1860s to provide chalk for the railway, the pit closed in 1902 and is now managed as a Nature Reserve by Yorkshire Wildlife Trust. It features several distinct habitats: the quarry floor, the steep chalk faces, and the original grassland above, making it home to a wide variety of wild flowers. These in turn support a great range of butterflies, at their best in July, when more than 20 species may be seen.

Among the various crops farmed locally, one of the most distinctive yet least familiar is borage. At a distance you may think that the purple-blue fields are growing lavender but at closer range the two plants are quite different. Borage is a sturdy plant, which produces star-shaped flowers. The young leaves were traditionally used in salads and the flowers are also edible, but it is principally grown as a source of oil, and has many uses in aromatherapy and herbal medicine; ancient wisdom has it that it will cheer you up and give you courage. It is not recommended to handle borage plants without gloves as they are covered in stiff, prickly hairs.

the ride

1 With your back to the road, turn right along the **railway track**. The actual riding surface is quite narrow, flanked by lush grass and then flowery banks, with lots of willowherb and scabious. Soon pass an access gate for **Kiplingcotes Chalk Pit** (the crumbling chalk faces can be seen by simply continuing along the track). Dip down through staggered barriers to cross a farm track where a bridge is missing, and up the other side to resume. The track soon leads out into a car park at the former Kiplingcotes station. There is an information board here and the **old signal box** is sometimes open as an information centre.

2 Keep straight on past the old platforms. Negotiate another set of barriers and dip, and shortly after cross the tarmac lane to **Wold Farm**. The views open out briefly but then it's back into a cutting – watch out for nettles and brambles. Go up a slight rise

2h00	10.75 MILES	17.3 KM	LEVEL 1 2 3

SHORTER ALTERNATIVE ROUTE

1h30	10 MILES	16.1 KM	LEVEL 1 2 3

MAP: OS Explorer 294 Market Weighton and Yorkshire Wolds Central

START/FINISH: Car park near Kiplingcotes Chalk Pit; grid ref: SE 909430

TRAILS/TRACKS: Old railway track, narrow in places; optional return on lanes

LANDSCAPE: rolling farmland with scattered woods

PUBLIC TOILETS: none on route

TOURIST INFORMATION: Beverley, tel 01482 867430

CYCLE HIRE: none locally

THE PUB: Light Dragoon, Etton

How to get to the start

Follow A1079 east from York, skirt round Market Weighton and climb up on to the Wolds. Turn left at the first cross-roads and follow the road down to a junction just before a bridge. Turn left then go for about 1.25 miles (2km) to a small car park on the right.

Why do this cycle ride?

To many people a rolling landscape of chalk hills, covered in broad fields and scattered woods, is quintessentially English. The Yorkshire Wolds produces gentle scenery, most of it given over to farming. The route follows the trackbed of a former railway line, which can be followed for the full distance of 11 or so miles (about 18km) from Market Weighton to Beverley. Those who want to avoid road riding entirely can ride it as an out-and-back route, but the suggested return through the lanes is very pleasant.

Researched and written by: Jon Sparks

to cross a lane and dip back down on to the **railway track**. Continue until it becomes necessary to drop down right, quite steeply, to a lane.

3 Cross and climb back up the other side on to the embankment. Soon there's a view ahead towards the village of Etton. Cross the track to **Etton Fields Farm**, and another field track shortly after. The following section can be quite muddy. (Those who are planning an out-and-back ride could turn round before the muddy section.) Where the shrouding trees fall back and the surroundings open out, look out for the stump of a **windmill** on the left. Just before a bridge over the track ahead, go right up a narrower track to a road.

4 Turn left, go over the bridge and follow the road straight down into the village

of **Etton**. At the T-junction turn left. **The Light Dragoon** is almost opposite.

5 Continue along the village street. Just after the **last houses** turn right, signposted for South Dalton, and up a short climb. Dead ahead as the gradient eases is the tall prominent spire of **St Mary's Church**, South Dalton. As the road begins to descend, turn left at a crossroads, signposted to Kiplingcotes and Market Weighton.

6 The road rolls along the crest of a broad ridge before a steeper descent leads down to an **angled crossroads**. Go left, signposted for Market Weighton, Kiplingcotes station and the Hudson Way. Just after passing a right turn to **Middleton-on-the-Wold**, turn left up the tarmac track that leads to Kiplingcotes station. Bear right back along the **railway track** to the start.

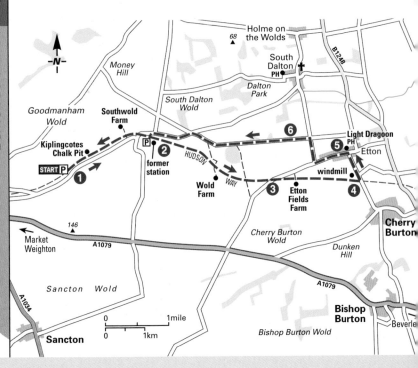

The Light Dragoon

is more extensive and may include Etton salad (black pudding, bacon and feta cheese), home-made steak pie with shortcrust pastry top, lasagne and prime steaks with sauces.

Family facilities
Children are made very welcome here. Youngsters have their own menu and some play equipment in the garden.

Alternative refreshment stops
None on route. Options in Cherry Burton.

☛ Where to go from here
Beverley and Market Weighton are both historic market towns and well worth exploring on foot. Visit the impressive Minster and enjoy a drink in the utterly unspoilt and candlelit White Horse Inn (Nellies) in Beverley.

Even if you don't plan on making the return through the lanes, it's not a problem to include this fine pub in your ride, as it's only about 0.5 mile (800m) from the nearest point on the railway track. It sits firmly at the centre of the charming village of Etton, which is not much more than one long street. The lounge bar is cosy and comfortable and some old wagon wheels incorporated into partitions are a notable feature. There's a separate dining room behind, housed in a modern extension that harmonises reasonably well with the original building. There's also a very pleasant garden, well away from road and car park, with swings and slide for the youngsters. On a summer evening the sky can be alive with swifts and swallows.

Food
At lunchtime tuck into various sandwiches, salads, pies and steak. The evening menu

about the pub

The Light Dragoon
Main Street, Etton
Beverley, East Yorkshire HU17 7PQ
Tel: 01430 810282

DIRECTIONS: Etton is located 1 mile (1.6km) off the B1248 north west of Beverley. Pub is on the right in the village centre opposite a road junction	
PARKING: 30	
OPEN: daily	
FOOD: daily, except Sunday evening	
BREWERY/COMPANY: Scottish Courage	
REAL ALE: Theakston XB & Black Bull	

Cleveland Way and Robin Hood's Bay

Through fields from this obscurely named village and back along part of the Cleveland Way.

Robin Hood's Bay

Walking the coastal path north of Robin Hood's Bay, you will notice how the sea is encroaching on the land. The route of the Cleveland Way has frequently to be redefined as sections slip into the sea. Around Robin Hood's Bay, the loss is said to be around 6 inches (15cm) every 2 years.

For countless visitors, Robin Hood's Bay is perhaps the most picturesque of the Yorkshire coast's fishing villages – a tumble of pantiled cottages that stagger down the narrow gully cut by the King's Beck. Narrow courtyards give access to tiny cottages, whose front doors look over their neighbours' roofs. Vertiginous stone steps link the different levels. Down at the shore, boats are still drawn up on the Landing, though they are more likely to be pleasure craft than working vessels.

There was a settlement where the King's Beck reaches the coast at least as far back as the 6th century. No one has yet put forward a convincing reason why this remote fishing village should bear Robin Hood's name – as it has since at least the start of the 16th century. Stories say that either Robin was offered a pardon by the Abbot of Whitby if he rid the east coast of pirates, or that, fleeing the authorities, he escaped arrest here disguised as a sailor.

the walk

1 From the lower car park opposite the **Victoria Hotel,** turn left up the hill and, where the road bends round to the left, take a signed footpath to the right over a stile. Walk up the fields over three stiles to a metalled lane.

2 Turn right. Go left through a **signed metal gate**. At the end of the field the path bends right to a gate in the hedge on your left. Continue down the next field with a stone wall on your left. Again, go right at the end of the field and over a stile into a green lane.

3 Cross to another waymarked stile and continue along the field edge with a wall

Large stones are strewn across the beach around Robin Hood's Bay

2h30 — **5.5 MILES** — **8.8 KM** — **LEVEL 123**

WALK

Robin Hood's Bay

NORTH YORKSHIRE

MAP: OS Explorer OL27 North York Moors – Eastern

START/FINISH: Car park at top of hill by the old railway station, Robin Hood's Bay; grid ref: NZ 950055

PATHS: field and coastal paths, a little road walking, 14 stiles

LANDSCAPE: farmland and fine coastline

PUBLIC TOILETS: at car park

TOURIST INFORMATION: Whitby, tel 01947 602674

THE PUB: The Victoria Hotel, Robin Hood's Bay

🛈 Take care on the road at the beginning of the walk. Keep well away from the friable cliff edges

Getting to the start

The old smugglers' village at Robin Hood's Bay huddles in a coastal hollow at the end of the B1447. It can be accessed from High Hawsker on the A171 Whitby to Scarborough road. There are two main car parks, both off to the right of the B road in the upper part of the village. The lower streets are access only.

Researched and written by:
John Gillham, David Winpenny

Far left: Narrow streets and alleys in Robin Hood's Bay are fronted by a jumble of houses

on your right. At the field end go over a stile on your right, then make for a **waymarked gate** diagonally left.

4 Walk towards the **Bottom House Farm**, through a gate and take the waymarked track round the right of the buildings to another gate, then to a waymarked opening beside a metal gate. Continue with a stone wall on your right, through another gate and on to a track that eventually bends left to a **waymarked stile**.

5 Continue to another stile, which leads to a **derelict footbridge** over a narrow beck. At a T-junction by a wooden electricity pylon, veer right and take a path to the right of the bank. After 50yds (46m), look for a signpost for **Hawsker** in woodland. Walk to the signpost then follow it right. As the hedge to your right curves left, go through a gap on the right and over a **signed stile**, walking straight ahead through the field to an opening by the main road.

6 Go right and right again, following the footpath sign, up the metalled lane towards two holiday parks. Pass **Seaview Caravan Park**, cross the former railway track and continue along the metalled lane, which bends right, goes downhill, crosses a stream and ascends to the **Northcliffe holiday park**.

7 Follow the footpath sign right, then go left and follow the metalled track down through the **caravans**, eventually leaving the track to go left to a waymarked path. Follow the path towards the **coastline**, to reach a signpost.

8 Turn right along the **Cleveland Way** for 2.5 miles (4km) alongside eroded shaly cliffs. At **Rocket Post Field** there's a minor waymarked **diversion** across fields to the right, caused by the cliff path collapsing into the sea. On the approach to Robin Hood's Bay go left through a gate and past

houses to reach the main road. Turn left for the lower car park and hotel.

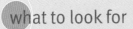

what to look for

At low tide, the bay reveals concentric arcs of rocks, the remains of a large rock dome that has, over the millennia, been eroded by the action of the sea. The ridges are bands of hard limestone and ironstone that have eroded less quickly than the softer lias between them. Where the lias is exposed fossil hunters search for shells (among them the characteristic whirls of the ammonites) and larger sea creatures.

The Victoria Hotel

Sited at the top of the village with fine views over the bay, this Victorian 'Gothic-style' building delivers more than first impressions promise, with fine food, hand-pulled Camerons beers and helpful courteous service. There is a family 'no smoking' room, simply but attractively furnished with bright warm colours – also an airy dining room with wood-panelled floor and huge panoramic windows overlooking the bay. Add ten pine-furnished en suite bedrooms, most with sea views, and you have a comfortable coastal retreat.

Food
Traditional food ranges from cold platters (cheese ploughman's with salad and pickles) and burgers to freshly battered Whitby haddock and chips, sausages and mash, steak pie, garlic chicken, sirloin steak with Stilton and white sauce, and home-made curries.

Family facilities
Families are made very welcome at this friendly inn. There's a family area downstairs and children have a good menu to choose from. Bedrooms include en suite family rooms.

Alternative refreshment stops
Stoke up in Robin Hood's Bay before the walk, as there is nowhere else on the route. In the village there are several pubs and cafés, including the Laurel Inn on New Road.

☛ Where to go from here
Travel south along the coast to Ravenscar, a headland where the Romans built a signal station. Alum shale, used in fixing, was mined here in the 17th and 18th centuries; you can see the scars of the industry and the Peak Alum Works explains more about the activity. Head north to Whitby and visit the town's fascinating museum (www.whitby-museum.org.uk) or enjoy a trip around Whitby harbour on board an authentic replica of Captain Cook's HMS *Endeavour*.

about the pub

The Victoria Hotel
Robin Hood's Bay, Whitby
North Yorkshire YO22 4RL
Tel: 01947 880205

DIRECTIONS: see Getting to the Start; pub opposite the car park	
PARKING: use village car park	
OPEN: daily; all day July and August	
FOOD: daily	
BREWERY/COMPANY: free house	
REAL ALE: Camerons Bitter & Strongarm, guest beer	
DOGS: in garden only	
ROOMS: 10 en suite	

From Ravenscar to Robin Hood's Bay

Fabulous views and a unique industrial heritage.

Alum Quarries

Just after the start of the railway track proper, you pass through an area of partly overgrown spoil heaps with quarried faces above. For around two centuries, up to the Victorian era, this was an internationally important source of alum (potassium aluminium sulphate). This chemical, known since at least Roman times, had many uses, notably in the fixing of dyes. The shale rock in the cliffs was rich in aluminium sulphate and it is reckoned that over a million tons of rock were removed. The manufacturing process was centred on the alum works. The best source of potassium was seaweed; however, to complete the reaction, ammonia was required, and

the best source of this was human urine! Much of this was shipped all the way from London and off-loaded on the rocky shores directly below – a trade with some unique hazards. It is said that proud sea-captains were reluctant to admit that they carried this undignified cargo, but if they were found out the cry would go up, 'You're taking the piss!' It's as good an explanation as any for the origins of the phrase. You can find out more about the alum industry at the Coastal Centre in Ravenscar.

the ride

1 Descend the road until it bends sharply right. Turn left, past the **National Trust Coastal Centre**, on to an obvious descending concrete track. A rougher section needs care, but lasts less than

A collection of red-roofed stone cottages stand on the cliffs above Robin Hood's Bay

— 2h00 — **11.25 MILES** **18.1 KM** — **LEVEL 1**23 —

MAP: OS Explorer OL27 North York Moors – Eastern

START/FINISH: roadside parking on way into Ravenscar; grid ref: NZ 980015

TRAILS/TRACKS: almost entirely on well-surfaced old railway track; short street sections at Ravenscar and Robin Hood's Bay

LANDSCAPE: steep cliffs and coastal slopes, woodland and farmland, sea views

PUBLIC TOILETS: at start

TOURIST INFORMATION: Whitby, tel 01947 602674

CYCLE HIRE: Trailways, Hawsker (about 3 miles from Robin Hood's Bay, on the railway route), tel 01947 820207

THE PUB: The Laurel Inn, Robin Hood's Bay

🛇 Busy roads and car park in Robin Hood's Bay village (possible to turn round before this)

How to get to the start
Turn off the A171 about midway between Whitby and Scarborough – signed for Ravenscar. Turn left at a T-junction, then right near an old windmill. The road descends into Ravenscar and there is extensive roadside parking as the descent gets steeper.

Why do this cycle ride?
The former railway line between Whitby and Scarborough can now be followed, in its entirety, on two wheels. The full distance is 20 miles (32.2km) one way, so this ride picks out probably the finest section, looping around Robin Hood's Bay. It is a little confusing that the name of the bay and the much-photographed village are exactly the same, but the ride gives great views of the former and a chance to visit the latter.

Researched and written by: Jon Sparks

100yds (91m). Swing left through a gate on to the old **railway trackbed** and a much easier surface.

2 The track now runs below the scarred face of the **alum workings,** with some ups and downs that clearly don't match the original rail contours exactly. After this, take care crossing a **steep concrete track** that runs down to a farm.

3 Pass under an **arched bridge**. Note more quarried cliffs up on the left, while looking down to the right – if the tide is not too high – there are extensive rocky platforms in the bay, with conspicuous parallel strata. There's a short cutting and the sea views are blocked by tall gorse and broom, then it becomes more open again as the track swings gradually inland. A tall embankment

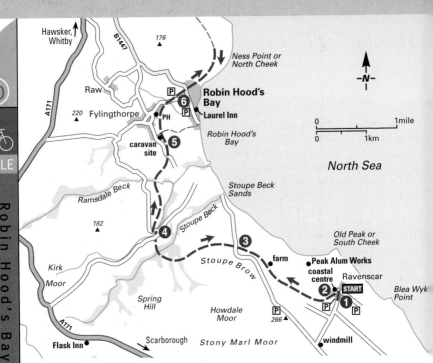

crosses a **steep wooded valley**. Go under a bridge and make a sharp left turn on to a lane.

4 Go up 20yds (18m) and then sharp right to the continuation of the track. Keep right at a fork and the track resumes its steady gentle descent, then starts to turn uphill for the first time. As you come into the open after a **tunnel of trees**, the direct way ahead is again blocked (unless you're Evel Knievel!). Slant down left, cross a lane, and then climb back up on to the continuing trackbed.

5 Pass a **cricket ground**, the back of a caravan site, then a farm. Cross the rough farm track and keep straight on, through a gate where the surface changes to tarmac, on the outskirts of Robin Hood's Bay. Go through another gate and drop down to a road. Turn right down this for 100yds (91m) then left on a lane signposted to **Station Workshops**. At the top of the rise is the old

station building and just beyond it a large car park. (It is, of course, possible to descend the road all the way into the village of Robin Hood's Bay, but it's a very steep climb back. An alternative is to lock the bikes at the car park and go down on foot.)

6 Continue alongside the car park, drop down to a road, turn left and almost instantly right (very nearly straight across) on to **Mount Pleasant**. Follow this to its end then bear left up a short gravelled ride to regain the railway path. Continue for about 0.5 mile (800m). There are good views back now over Robin Hood's Bay to the cliffs near Ravenscar. Look for a National Trust sign for **Ness Bay**. There is open access on foot so you could leave the bikes and walk down to the headland, a great picnic spot. This makes as good a turn-round point as any, though the track continues into Hawsker and on to Whitby.

The Laurel Inn

The picturesque fishing village of Robin Hood's Bay is the setting for this delightful little pub. Tucked away in a row of fishermen's cottages at the bottom of the village overlooking the sea, the pub retains lots of character features, including beams and an open fire. The traditional bar is decorated with old photographs of the area, Victorian prints and brasses and an international collection of lager bottles. This coastal village was once the haunt of smugglers who used a network of underground tunnels and secret passages to bring the booty ashore.

Food
Bar food is limited to a simple and straightforward menu offering wholesome sandwiches and soups.

Family facilities
Due to its size there are few facilities for family groups although children are very welcome in the snug bar until 9pm.

Alternative refreshment stops
Various pubs and cafés in Robin Hood's Bay including The Victoria Hotel at the top of the village.

☛ Where to go from here
Locally, learn more about alum mining at the Peak Alum Works in Ravenscar and this fascinating coastline at the Ravenscar Coastal Centre. Children will enjoy visiting the Old Coastguard Station in Robin Hood's Bay. Head north to Whitby to see the moody and magnificent ruins of Whitby Abbey (www.english-heritage.org.uk) and visit the Captain Cook Memorial Museum

about the pub

The Laurel Inn
New Road, Robin Hood's Bay
North Yorkshire YO22 4SE
Tel: 01947 880400

DIRECTIONS: bottom of the village
PARKING: use village car park
OPEN: daily; all day (2pm–11pm Monday to Friday November to February)
FOOD: daily
BREWERY/COMPANY: free house
REAL ALE: Adnams Broadside, Tetley, Jennings Cumberland

(www.cookmuseumwhitby.co.uk). High on the list for children may be the Sea Life and Marine Sanctuary in Scarborough, home to seahorses, otters, sharks, a seal hospital and convalescing sea turtles.

Acknowledgements

The Automobile Association would like to thank the following photo library, photographers and establishments for their assistance in the preparation of this book.

Photolibrary.com front cover b.
John Gilham 27, 31, 35, 36/7, 39, 47, 51, 63, 69, 71, 72, 75, 82, 83, 87, 95, 107, 119, 123, 127, 131, 144, 159, 160, 162, 171; Jon Sparks 55, 91tl, 100, 103, 167.
Blacksmiths Arms, Lastingham 143; Devonshire Arms, Skipton 67; The George & Dragon, Aysgarth 59; Stone Trough Inn, Whitewell-on-the-Hill 147.

The remaining photographs are held in the Automobile Associations's own Photo Library (AA World Travel Library) and were taken by the following photographers:

Adrian Baker 42; Peter Baker 84; Pete Bennett 136; E A Bowness 12; Stephen Gregory 151, 169; Tom Mackie 15; S & O Mathews 20/1, 24, 25, 77; John Morrison front cover cl, ccl, cr, 4, 17tl, 17br, 19, 34, 56, 61, 65, 73, 82. 83, 87, 88/9, 91br, 97, 108, 109, 111, 112, 113, 115, 121, 122, 124, 126, 128, 129, 133, 135, 138, 139, 141, 142, 152, 153, 155, 158, 164, 168, 172/3; Rich Newton 116, 117; Graham Rowatt 149; Stephen Gregory 151, 168/9; Tony Souter 14b; David Tarn front cover ccr, 28, 29, 32, 52, 64, 76; Wyn Voysey 13, 14t, 50; Linda Whitwam 45, 92/3, 104; Peter Wilson 36, 57, 68/9, 81.